FOREWORD BY STEPHEN M.R. COVEY

SEEING
the
BIG
PICTURE

BUSINESS ACUMEN to BUILD YOUR
CREDIBILITY, CAREER, *and* COMPANY

KEVIN COPE
Founder of Acumen Learning

GREENLEAF
BOOK GROUP PRESS

Published by Greenleaf Book Group Press
Austin, Texas
www.gbgpress.com

Distributed by Greenleaf Book Group LLC

For ordering information or special discounts for bulk purchases, please contact Greenleaf Book Group LLC at PO Box 91869, Austin, TX 78709, 512.891.6100.

Design and composition by Greenleaf Book Group LLC
Cover design by Greenleaf Book Group LLC

Publisher's Cataloging-In-Publication Data
(Prepared by The Donohue Group, Inc.)
Cope, Kevin, 1962-
  Seeing the big picture : business acumen to build your credibility, career and com-
pany / Kevin Cope. — 1st ed.
    p. : ill., charts ; cm.
  Includes bibliographical references.
  ISBN: 978-1-60832-246-6
  1. Success in business. 2. Career development. 3. Executive ability. 4. Strategic
planning—Employee participation. I. Title.
HF5386 .C66 2012
650.1   2011940662

Part of the Tree Neutral® program, which offsets the number of
trees consumed in the production and printing of this book by taking
proactive steps, such as planting trees in direct proportion to the
number of trees used: www.treeneutral.com

TreeNeutral

Printed in the United States of America on acid-free paper

14 15 16 17 18 19   10 9 8 7 6 5 4

First Edition

CONTENTS

*Dedicated to my wife, Karen, and our children,
who are truly the greatest joy of my life.*

FOREWORD

I strongly believe that the first job of any leader is to inspire trust. Whether that leader is a surgeon leading a team through an intricate medical procedure, an executive leading a team in implementing a strategy, or a quarterback leading a football team to a comeback victory—it's trust in the leader that inspires others to willingly choose to follow.

So what inspires trust? Trust is the confidence that emerges when character and competence converge. If I were questioning whether or not I needed surgery, I wouldn't trust a dishonest and self-serving surgeon—no matter how competent he or she might be. Nor would I trust a quarterback who's unable to make plays or deliver results—even if he has impeccable character. But when I see the consistent demonstration of both character and competence, I do trust. And Kevin Cope, the author of this exceptional book, is a person who consistently demonstrates both—and is a person I trust immensely.

Kevin is a long-time friend and confidant. As such, he listens empathically and offers sound advice when I ask for it. He is also a business colleague who worked with me for several years in a time of unprecedented business growth, opportunity, and challenge. In that role, I have seen him time and again roll up his sleeves and find a way to get the job done superbly well. While I wouldn't trust Kevin to quarterback a fourth quarter comeback (believe me, I've played flag football with him!), and I definitely wouldn't trust him to perform surgery on me (he's not a doctor), I absolutely do trust Kevin's ideas on business, organizations, and people. He's earned that trust through a demonstrated track record of character and competence—particularly in the area of business acumen.

In fact, it is because of my trust in Kevin in these areas that I strongly encouraged him to write this book. His "five drivers" model and his ideas concerning business are simply too good—too valuable, too insightful, too clear—to not share. Kevin has the gift of being able to take complex issues and make them simple. Never is this gift more needed than in the world of business acumen, particularly regarding how business works and how organizations make money and successfully grow. And when it comes to understanding how business acumen can transform an individual—and, in turn, an organization—there is *no one* I trust more than Kevin Cope.

But enough said about my friend Kevin; now let's talk about you. You're picking up this book because you likely work for a business or for some type of organization that needs to operate on sound business principles. Now just because a person works for a business doesn't mean he or she fully understands business. You and I both know plenty of bright business graduates who can't quite seem to apply that knowledge in relevant ways that create value for the business. We've all run across colleagues and peers who have years of experience and know everything there is to know about their particular function—HR, operations, marketing, sales, R & D, or some other role—but who would rather have a root canal than to have to give an opinion or interpretation of the company's latest financial results.

We're also aware of those who think they know business when all they really know is the jargon of business—often number crunchers who, as Oscar Wilde put it, "know the price of everything but the value of nothing." We likewise see countless passionate entrepreneurs who are certain they understand business, but start companies that fail to gain any traction and end up not even getting off the ground.

In short, just because a person is "in" business doesn't mean that person "gets" business. That's where this book comes in. It's the best book I know to explain how business really works and how organizations make money. It's actionable. It's *simple* without being *simplistic*. And it's written in an engaging and insightful style.

So if you're that business grad or entrepreneur who can't put your finger on why success seems to elude you . . . or that functional expert with years of experience who's tired of being overlooked when your company presents new career opportunities . . . or that numbers person who's wrestling with how you can become relevant to those who don't look at the numbers in the same way you do . . . or—like me—an executive who's looking for a quick reference field guide to help you focus your team on the simple fundamentals of business success . . . this book is for you.

Whatever your situation—and whether you're just getting started in business, trying to get reenergized about your business, or actually running a business—I strongly encourage you to read *Seeing the Big Picture* and carefully consider what Kevin has to say. I am convinced that doing so will help you become a more competent businessperson. And if you combine that competence with strong character, you'll inspire your peers, your team, your boss or your CEO, to trust your decisions. They'll come to see you not only as a leader of people, but also as a leader of the business. And that's what good business acumen is all about.

Stephen M. R. Covey, author of
New York Times bestseller *The Speed of Trust*

INTRODUCTION

The only real security that a person will have in this world is a reserve of knowledge, experience, and ability.
—*Henry Ford*

Everything should be made as simple as possible, but not simpler.
—*Albert Einstein*

Have you ever found yourself in one of these situations?

You're talking with a senior leader of your company and wish you could say something really insightful to show your knowledge of the business, but your brain goes numb and you can't come up with anything meaningful.

You're attending a meeting with managers or financial types and as they start reviewing financial statements, you get lost. You hope no one discovers that the smile on your face or the nod of your head hides the gap in your knowledge. You can't see what the numbers have to do with what you have to get done today or this week.

Your CEO wants everyone to work harder to meet the company's overall financial objectives. Your manager asks for ideas from the team, but you're struggling to see how improving your job performance will impact the company's revenue or stock price.

You've got a great idea for a weekend business that you and a friend or your spouse could start up to bring in some extra money, but you don't know how much money you would need to get started or how to handle financial matters once you do. You just don't want to be like all those other start-ups that flop.

If you've experienced moments like these, you certainly are not alone. In fact, you're a member of a fairly large group—businesspeople who struggle to understand how the moving parts of a company work together to make it successful *and* how financial metrics like profit margin, cash flow, and stock price reflect how well each of those moving parts is doing its job.

The solution to your confusion is developing your *business acumen*, your ability to see the big picture.

WHAT BUSINESS ACUMEN CAN DO FOR YOU

Years ago a colleague of mine was consulting with a group of senior NASA managers at Cape Canaveral. He tried to explain, in simple terms, an organizational change strategy. The managers seemed confused. In an effort to clarify, he said, "Please don't make this more complicated than it is. It's not rocket science." To which they sincerely answered, "We wish it were. We'd understand it better!"

Many people, even those with jobs that others think of as incredibly complex, view their business much like rocket science: a lot of complexity, hard-to-understand data and formulas, communications in a language that barely resembles English. Yet most of them wish they could more clearly understand the business of their business and how to help their companies perform better. What they are wishing for is business acumen.

Business acumen is keen, fundamental, street-smart insight into how your business operates and how it makes money and sustains profitable growth, now and in the future.

In 2002, after ten years as an executive with FranklinCovey, consulting with and teaching for dozens of organizational clients, I founded my own training and consulting firm, Acumen Learning. We created and began delivering the Building Business Acumen® seminar. Over the last ten years we have expanded and deepened the initial course. Our focus became the practical application of business acumen to help people—at all levels, in any company, in any industry—become more effective in their current jobs and more successful in their future careers.

After working with more than one hundred thousand participants in more than thirty countries, including many clients in the Fortune 500 and eighteen of the Fortune 50, the primary lesson we've learned is that businesspeople *want* to become more effective and valuable, to secure their seat at the table and influence decisions, to impact company performance. They want to use their full potential to help their business make money and sustain profitable growth.

They want these things for two reasons. First, we all instinctively seek out greater engagement—a way to feel that the work we do is worthwhile and makes a difference. Second, they understand something crucial. If you want to be in a better position—a job you like more with better pay, better long-term opportunities, and greater security, for example—you need to understand the key drivers of business and use that knowledge to make good things happen.

To do that, you need the ability to

1. See the "big picture" of your organization—how the key drivers of your business relate to each other, work together to produce profitable growth, and relate to the job you do each day

2. Understand important company communications and data, including financial statements

3. Use your knowledge to make good decisions

4. Understand how your actions and decisions impact key company measures and the objectives of your company's leadership

5. Effectively communicate your ideas to other employees, managers, and executives

For some of you, this list might resonate immediately. For others, it might raise an important question. *Why should you care?* Isn't making these connections the responsibility of the executives, the senior leadership, or maybe your boss? Not if you want to be doing something different and better in your career three years from now.

If, through your questions, ideas, comments, analysis, proposals, and performance, you exhibit business acumen, you will be seen as a more valuable contributor. You will demonstrate your worth to the company, and other people will notice.

And that, in a nutshell, is the path to success in almost any career.

THE BIG PICTURE

Robert was an excellent call center supervisor . . . or so he thought. He was dedicated to saving the company money because he was worried that they would outsource the call center to an overseas operation. He rarely recommended employees for recognition or raises. If his team presented ideas about new software or equipment that could improve productivity, he would listen but never take them to management for consideration. And he constantly harped on the importance of getting through calls as quickly as possible and up-selling customers as much as possible. He was fanatical about doing his job well.

Robert didn't realize that his narrow focus on cost control and "doing his job well" ignored the big picture of how his company made money and sustained profitability. He wasn't connecting the dots between his efforts, customer relations, and future sales revenue. Or the huge cost of employee turnover the company was incurring every time one of his employees left to go somewhere with better pay and a stronger focus on serving customers. He failed to consider the impact he had on efficiency, profits, and morale by refusing to raise his team's ideas with management.

Ultimately, Robert was viewed by senior management as "a serviceable supervisor in need of development; not likely management material." While he wasn't let go, his performance reviews were never stellar and he could tell that he was being sidelined, but he didn't understand why. Robert missed out on seeing the big picture of his *main job*: to contribute to building a company experiencing long-term, sustainable, profitable growth.

So many of us fall into the same trap. Like Robert, over time, we tend to become more specialized and get very good at focusing on the specific parts of our jobs, so much so that we fail to see the big picture—how what we do fits into the overall picture of helping the company make money, achieve its strategic objectives, and be profitable.

Some of us decide to get degrees in management, hoping to get that big-picture perspective. But while management education provides excellent training in areas such as accounting, marketing, or finance, students can graduate without an overall knowledge of how a business runs successfully. Their knowledge of the key drivers of business and how they work together can be fragmented, disjointed from the reality of daily operations.

And as with Robert's managers, many leaders assume that their teams have a much stronger grasp of the big picture of how their companies grow profitably—greater business acumen—than they actually do, so few take the time to do on-the-job training to deepen that knowledge.

Do you think you're better off than Robert? That you wouldn't have made the same mistakes? Now's your chance to prove it. Take the Big Picture Quick Quiz shown here. The questions were not picked at random; they are the result of research and interviews with hundreds of executives and CEOs from dozens of different industries. They reflect the areas of performance that senior leaders have on their minds and want employees to have on theirs.

We've administered the Big Picture Quick Quiz to over sixty thousand people. On average, people know the answer to *fewer than two of the questions.*

These questions focus on the overall business, not the operations of your department or division. I suspect that you might be more familiar with some of the performance measures for your immediate team. But your senior management team wants the entire business to be profitable, *not* just a single unit. They want all employees to understand and better contribute to how the entire company makes money.

THE BIG PICTURE QUICK QUIZ

Answer the following questions based on your company's performance in the *most recent fiscal year*. And don't look up the answers!

1. How much cash was on hand at year-end?
2. How much cash was generated from operations?
3. What was the net income (net earnings, or net profit)?
4. What was the net profit (net income, or net earnings) margin?
5. What was the total revenue (or total sales)?
6. What was the inventory turnover (for retail and manufacturing firms)?
7. What was your return on assets?
8. By what percentage did total revenue (sales) grow or decline over the previous year?
9. By what percentage did net income (net earnings, or net profit) grow or decline over the previous year?
10. How do your results compare to your competition?

Now check your answers against any of the financial reports you have on hand. How did you do? How many questions did you get right? Do you even know where to get this information?

The problem is that while we understand our jobs, the big picture seems too complex to grasp. Complexity is an underlying challenge in any business, regardless of size, industry, or stage of development. Large companies, especially, have many moving parts—departments and divisions (always reorganizing), product lines (always changing), layers of management, competitive realities, unclear decision-making processes, regulatory pressure, shifting budgets, new strategies. A small problem within any single element might produce a ripple effect throughout the organization, requiring major repairs. But without knowing the true source of the difficulty (which is not always readily identifiable), we might "fix" the wrong thing as we tinker with the business.

Developing business acumen helps us cut through this complexity, get a bird's eye view of a business, and understand our specialized roles within it. Simplifying complexity and broadening our understanding of the business enables us to fix present problems, prevent new ones, and take advantage of opportunities to grow.

How do we simplify the complex? By looking at the key drivers that make all the parts of a business run.

THE 5 KEY DRIVERS OF ANY BUSINESS

When you break down even the largest, most complex multinational company—like Walmart, Apple, Toyota, or Boeing—into its most fundamental elements, you'll find the same drivers that power your business, or *any* business. What are those drivers?

- Cash
- Profit
- Assets
- Growth
- People

How did we distill it down to these five? We used the core financial statements—the statement of cash flows (cash), the income statement (profit), and the balance sheet (assets)—as the foundation. These are the statements every company uses to judge its current strength and its future prospects. The fourth driver, growth, is reflected in all of these statements and for public companies is an important objective for shareholders. And the fifth driver is quite simple: without good employees providing value to paying customers, the other four drivers cease to exist.

The 5 Key Drivers will help you understand and visualize how even the most complicated business can be analyzed and improved. Like the twenty-six characters of the English alphabet, the 5 Key Drivers combine in a multitude of ways to form the foundation of organization, products, market position, financing, human resources, and every other strategy or decision in a company. Leaders must set and achieve goals and obtain results in these five areas in order to achieve the most important objective for any company: long-term, sustainable profitability to support its mission.

You've probably heard of these essential elements, but you may not really understand their full importance and interdependence in creating success. While each driver is unique, it is also completely dependent on all of the other drivers, as shown in the model. You cannot affect one without influencing the performance of another. Leaders have to take the connections between the drivers into account as they make their decisions, or they risk becoming overly focused on one driver and running a business into the ground.

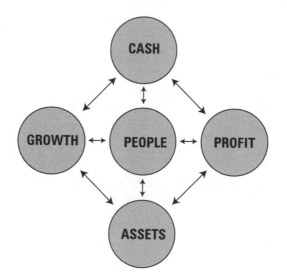

Your ability to understand these relationships and affect these drivers through your decisions and actions can increase your own ability to contribute to the long-term profitability and growth of your company. So in chapters 1 through 5, I will explore each of the five drivers in depth, explaining how they are defined, their importance to a business, how leaders balance each of the drivers as they work toward strategic goals, and how any employee can influence them. In chapter 6, I'll look at the big picture the five drivers create; how they relate to each other and work together to create sustainable, profitable growth; and how they are influenced by factors in the broader business environment. Management's general objective is to achieve a balance among the drivers; supreme focus on one and neglect of the others can be disastrous over time. Throughout the book, I'll offer up real-world stories to help you understand what the drivers may mean to your business, and I'll use the hypothetical story of Austin's Cycle Shop to deepen your understanding of how the drivers play out in a business month to month and year to year.

A key component of business acumen is being able to communicate about the 5 Key Drivers. The language of business is accounting and finance. And this means numbers. And numbers intimidate many people. But if you think of financial statements like you would a health report from your doctor, you may not be as intimidated. You don't need to understand every number or how it was calculated, but recognizing a critical few pieces of information, those that reflect the 5 Key Drivers, will help you understand the health of any company.

While business acumen is more than just accounting, an important part of it is understanding a company's "financials." So in chapter 7 I'll explain how financial statements work, and in chapters 8 through 10 I'll take the three most important financial statements—the income statement, the balance sheet, and the statement of cash flows—and de-intimidate them, simplify them. I'll show how these three financials measure the 5 Key Drivers and how they describe the real-world performance of your company. You'll be able to look for and understand only the most important data and not be concerned with the rest of the complexity.

I encourage you to explore our website www.seeingthebigpicture. com, which offers tools, resources, and further education to help you continue to develop your business acumen.

INFLUENCING THE WHOLE

If you want to be more visible and valued, demonstrate that you understand how your department or unit fits into the big picture of the overall business.

If you want to influence the thinking and decisions of your supervisor or manager, address the topics that senior leaders, including your boss, are concerned about. Communicate your ideas and proposals in language that he or she understands.

If you want to be seen as a major contributor, show that you understand the relationships among the key drivers of your overall business—not just how *your* department works.

If you want to be a more effective leader, better able to engage your team, link your team's actions with the overall needs and strategic goals of the company. Keep in mind, even your managers might not be as knowledgeable in some of these areas as you think. While they may be functionally brilliant, they may not see the big picture. But I encourage you to ask questions of the type raised in this book and be willing to act on the answers. You'll be recognized as a contributor, somebody who demonstrates business acumen through savvy questions and effective actions.

I hope you'll refer to the book and the resources in it often and apply them in your present job and throughout your future career.

PART I

Key Drivers of Any Business and
How to Influence Them

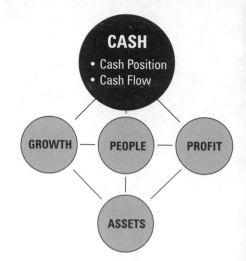

Chapter 1

CASH

The only unforgivable sin in business is to run out of cash.
—Harold Geneen

My wife and I were raising four children, all wonderful boys, when she was diagnosed with cancer. The treatment worked and she is doing well today, but the doctors told us that she wouldn't be able to have any more children. We had been hoping for a daughter to round out our family, so we decided to adopt. Eventually, we welcomed a darling baby girl into our lives. You might suspect what happened next. Soon after finalizing the adoption, my wife got pregnant—with a little girl. So now we have an amazing family of eight.

The process of adoption inspired us with an idea. One day, we would like to start an organization that helps families through the adoption process, which can take much time, money, and patience.

Every day, people are inspired to fulfill a need they see in the market or the world by starting a business. What about you? I'm sure that in your life you've had lots of ideas for businesses or products or services. Maybe it's just a hobby, or maybe you have grander entrepreneurial dreams. Ask yourself this question: What is the one thing you would need to actually launch your business?

A marketable product or service? Time? Drive? Well, yes, but they will not necessarily get you out of the gates.

What you really need to start and sustain almost any business is cash.

Cash is the fuel that drives a business. Without cash, a business can't pay its bills, can't pay its employees, can't buy the goods it needs to produce the products or services it sells, can't generate revenue or profit. Without cash, eventually a company will go out of business. And with a reasonable amount of cash on hand or the ability to easily get more, a company can weather tough market and economic storms, can grow by investing in new software or research or equipment, can take advantage of new market opportunities, and can even buy out competitors.

A business must have cash to survive and thrive.

THE IMPORTANCE OF CASH

In 2008, major companies such as Bear Stearns, Lehman Brothers, General Motors, Fannie Mae, Freddie Mac, and at least twenty-two major banks either went bankrupt, were purchased cheaply, or ran to the government for a bailout because they did not have adequate cash. They each experienced a severe *liquidity* crisis.

Large, well-known companies like these, who most people believed were "too big to fail," developed serious cash problems through a series of events. First, because of their own financial mismanagement, they failed to generate enough cash through operations to pay the bills. When this happens, a company usually borrows money from a bank or financial institution. But that option wasn't available to these organizations. Their poor financial situations significantly lowered their credit ratings, making them high-risk borrowers. And financial institutions were developing liquidity problems of their own due, in large part, to bad loan portfolios, so they didn't have cash to lend. Their next option was to seek out cash from investors, but the markets were starting to get shaky, and investors were wary of companies that were already showing signs of weakness.

Thus began the series of bailouts, buyouts, and bankruptcies.

Why does cash play such an important role in the life of a business? Let's consider the role of cash in your life. You use cash (or checks or a debit card) every day to pay for your rent or mortgage, food, doctor visits, your cell phone bill, and cappuccinos. If you pay bills with your credit card, you are borrowing cash that the credit card company sends to the vendor. You make investments with cash. You even pay for large purchases like your home or vehicles with cash: What cash you don't pay directly from your own funds, you borrow from a bank or other lender in the form of a loan.

Likewise, all businesses—from giants like Walmart, Citibank, and Microsoft to the small neighborhood flower shops or mom-and-pop diners—need cash to pay their bills and other obligations. According to a U.S. Small Business Administration study, only 44 percent of small businesses survive at least four years, and one of the primary reasons is inadequate capitalization—too little cash. Without cash, a business will fail, so business owners and leaders often find creative ways to get it when times are tough.

Fred Smith, who founded Federal Express at age twenty-seven in 1971, is a great example. In a 1979 interview, Smith said, "People thought we were bananas. We were too ignorant to know that we weren't supposed to be able to do certain things" (*New York Times*, January 7, 1979). Federal Express's first two years were grim. In fact, on its first night of business, the fledgling company shipped only 186 packages on its fourteen Falcon jets routed to twenty-two cities. It was not uncommon for Federal Express drivers to dig into their own pockets to pay for gas. Despite his $84 million in start-up capital (another term for cash), *Business Week* reported that within a few months of delivering his first packages in March 1973, Smith was desperate for cash. The challenges and risks of starting a major global business were significant. Federal regulations were severely hampering his efforts to compete with the U.S. Postal Service. Suddenly, he didn't even have enough cash to pay a jet fuel bill, and if he didn't pay the supplier, FedEx would be unable to fly planes or pay employees. So what did he do? He went to Las Vegas and played the blackjack tables. He wired $27,000 back to his FedEx headquarters and the employees got paid . . . and you know the rest of the story.

I wouldn't recommend using the blackjack strategy to get cash for your business—or your life! But it's tempting for people and businesses to take risks when they need cash now to ensure their future survival.

AKA

Other terms or phrases people use when they are talking about cash are *cash and cash equivalents*, *cash on hand*, *cash available*, *cash balance*, *capital*, and *money*.

MEASURING A COMPANY'S CASH AND LIQUIDITY

In order to evaluate a company's ability to survive and grow even in difficult economic times—its financial strength—we can look at three components of cash:

1. How much cash does the company currently have available, immediately? This is called its *cash position*.

2. How much cash will it generate and spend through its operations during a given period? This is called *cash flow*.

3. In addition to a company's cash position, how quickly and inexpensively could it generate more cash by selling assets? This is called *liquidity*.

Those in business and finance—investors, banks, shareholders, vendors—measure a company's cash position in relationship to its financial obligations—how much it has versus how much it owes—and its track record of generating cash flow from operations.

If you think about it, these are the same concerns you have about your own financial situation. How much do you have in your bank accounts and how much do you owe every month? How sure are you that you'll get more cash next month? If you lost your job or other income, would you be able to keep paying your bills? I hope you can see how the second question in particular is directly tied to the liquidity of the company you work for. If its financial situation is unstable, how long can it support yours? This is a good reason to pay attention to these issues.

Cash Position

Usually, when businesspeople use the term *cash*, they are referring to a company's cash position—the amount of cash a business has at any single point in time, which, for public companies, is reported at the end of a quarter or at the close of its fiscal year.

But how is that number calculated? Is it just a lump sum sitting in a bank account somewhere? Not quite.

The most obvious factor in determining the cash position is actual *cash on hand*, which includes currency, coin, and checks in hand—on the premises—but not yet deposited. It also includes cash balances in accounts of all types at banks and other financial institutions.

The second part of the equation is *cash equivalents*: any short-term securities or other financial instruments, such as stock market or money market investments, certificates of deposit, or short-term treasury bills, that can be sold or converted to cash quickly, usually within ninety days.

You can't pay bills with money you don't have yet, so a company's cash position does *not* include accounts receivable—money owed to a company from customers who purchased goods or services on credit. Accounts receivable represent cash to be collected in the *future*, but your cash position is the cash that can be spent *now*.

Cash Flow

Companies rich in cash exemplify the saying "Cash is king!" However, it is not only the amount of cash a company has on hand *now*, but also a company's ability to generate cash flow in the future, that is important. As the financial columnist Jim Jubak says, "Cash cows are kings."

Many investors, financial analysts, and company leaders consider cash flow to be the most important indicator of a company's financial health and strength—its ability to be successful and make money over the long term. Many, including the late Peter Drucker, consider cash flow to be even more important than profit.

Cash flow is simply the volume of cash that *flows through* a business as a result of operations over a period of time. The two factors of cash flow are cash inflows, which is cash received in the form of sales, and cash outflows, or the expenses the company must pay as its various moving parts perform their functions. Simply put, cash flow is cash received less cash paid out as part of the core business operations. A company can have either a *positive cash flow*—total cash inflows are greater than total cash outflows—or a *negative cash flow*—outflows are greater than inflows.

You can see why investors, shareholders, and employees should be concerned about a company that is consistently paying out more cash than it's bringing in. That company probably isn't profitable in the short term, and if it can't adjust its operations to bring in more cash, it will eventually be unable to pay its bills and be forced to declare bankruptcy or close its doors.

Let's meet Austin and his cycle shop to see how cash position and cash flow actually play out in a business.

Austin's Cycle Shop

A few years ago Austin opened his own bicycle sales and service shop—called Austin's Cycle Shop. He determined that he needed $50,000 to get up and running, so he used money from his own savings and borrowed money from a bank and a private investor, his brother-in-law. Start-up costs—his store lease, professional fees, licenses, furnishings for the store, inventory (bikes and parts), and equipment—were $40,000. He put the remaining $10,000 in the bank as a safety net for the early months when sales and revenue might be shaky. So his initial cash position was $10,000.

But during the first year, Austin collected $70,000 from selling and servicing bicycles. He also had expenses of $55,000 (he took a very small salary that first year). So how much cash did he generate from his operations? What was his cash flow? Right, $15,000. He never touched his initial cash reserves, so at the end of year 1, he had a total cash position of $25,000 ($10,000 + $15,000).

In his second year, he received $100,000 in cash from sales and spent $80,000 in operating his business, so he generated $20,000 in cash flow.

An important note: Cash flow is not profit. In the next chapter we'll look at the profit a company makes in relationship to its ability to generate significant cash flows and how they are different.

Liquidity

When we talk about how *liquid* a company is, we are referring to its cash position plus its ability to generate cash quickly and without much cost by selling its assets. (To *liquidate* means to sell assets to turn them into cash.) By definition, cash and cash equivalents are the most liquid assets. But that doesn't mean that a company that doesn't have a lot of cash on hand is illiquid. Walmart, for example, consistently carries relatively (*relatively* being a key word here) low balances of cash and cash equivalents, yet it is still a very liquid company. Why? Because it also carries large amounts of inventory that it is constantly converting into cash—it has a strong ability to generate substantial cash flow through rapid inventory turnover.

On the other hand, if a company did not have large amounts of cash and owned mostly *fixed assets*—assets such as real estate and office buildings that could take months or even years to sell at uncertain prices—it would be considered less liquid. If that company couldn't show that it had the ability to generate solid cash flow, investors and stockholders would start to worry.

If we want a deeper understanding of cash and how a company actually generates it, we have to look at all the ways a company gets cash and uses it.

HOW COMPANIES GET AND USE CASH

There are three types of activities in which companies participate to either get or use cash. Each of the following activities is a source of cash for a company but also requires it to disburse cash. The hope for any company is that it gets more than it uses.

Operating activities: Cash generated from your company's core business activities less the cash expenses from those activities is its cash flow or cash from operations, as we just discussed. Operating activities are the most important source of cash because they are the activities the company engages in to make money (like selling bicycles, for instance) and therefore should be an ongoing source of cash. Simply put, you *get* cash from sales and you *use* cash for expenses to determine cash flow from operating activities.

Investing activities: Investing activities require a company to use cash to purchase things like equipment or facilities (vehicles, computers, warehouses), real estate, stocks or bonds (securities), and other businesses through mergers and acquisitions. A company uses cash in this way because it believes that it will be able to either use the assets it invests in to create more cash flow as part of its core business, or earn interest or dividends or be able to sell the investment for more money than it paid for it. Investing activities are necessary for most businesses, but they come with a bit of risk because a return on the investment (cash in greater than cash out) is not a guarantee.

A company can sell existing assets (like buildings or equipment) to generate cash, but that isn't a sustainable way to get cash, primarily because you wouldn't have use of the asset anymore. It would be like a carpenter selling his tools to raise money. While he got cash in the short-term, he has reduced his ability to generate cash in the future. After the Gulf oil spill of 2010, British Petroleum investors began to worry that the company would divest itself of too many valuable assets, trapping them in an organization with increasingly fewer cash-generating holdings. After BP divested itself of $7 billion in assets, investor concerns presented themselves in the increase of the oil company's interest paid on debt, according to the *Guardian* ("What will BP sell next?," July 22, 2010); yields on five-year dollar bonds jumped to a sky-high 8 percent at the height of the panic (they'd been at 3 percent before the spill).

Financing activities: A company can get cash through financing activities by borrowing from financial institutions or investors or selling shares of company stock. Conversely, it may use cash in these activities by paying back loans, paying dividends to stockholders, or buying back shares of company stock. For more information on why this might occur, see chapter 6 or go to our website (www.seeingthebigpicture.com).

Cash received and used in each of these three areas is tracked on a company's statement of cash flows, which shows sources of cash (where it comes from) and how cash is used (where it goes). I'll discuss the statement of cash flows in chapter 10. Again, cash generated from operations (the core business) is the best source of cash because your company doesn't have to sell assets (investing activities) or borrow money (financing activities).

Overall, the formula for determining how much cash has been generated through any of these activities is:

$$\text{Cash in} - \text{Cash out} = \text{Cash generated}$$

So to keep the amount of cash generated positive and growing, companies want to increase the "cash in" at a greater rate than the "cash out" as they grow overall.

Generating More Cash

Most companies are interested in generating more cash, even if they already have a strong cash position and cash flow. Improving operating cash flow in particular is a sign that the company is doing well and should continue to do well, at least in the near term.

So how might your company work to generate more cash?

Fundamentally, it will start with operations and try to increase revenues (cash in) or reduce expenses (cash out). From there, it will invest in resources or assets, like two new ovens to cook more pizzas faster, that it can use to generate more cash flow. And if it needs money for a big strategic initiative, like opening five new stores, it will seek financing.

Businesses may also attempt to bring in cash more quickly than they expend it. This supplies the company with immediate cash and may eliminate the need for borrowing (and thus the expense of interest). Dell's cash flow strategy is to collect money from the customer for orders placed over the phone or Internet before it builds or ships the product. The company then negotiates with its suppliers to pay them two to three months later, providing Dell with plenty of cash on hand to meet its short-term obligations.

But the goal for any business is to generate as much cash as possible from operations now and in the future.

What does this mean for you? Depending upon your role in your company, you will have different opportunities to impact cash. For example, if you're in sales or marketing, you can help generate more cash faster by increasing sales revenue. If you work directly with customers, you can provide excellent service so that customers are more likely to continue buying from the company. If you're in accounting, you might negotiate longer payment terms with suppliers (but be careful that you don't negatively impact the relationship or give up discounts for early payment) to hold on to cash as long as possible. Or you might work to make sure more customers pay their bills on time or early. If you're part of the financial management staff, you might be responsible for looking for better financing terms on loans for new equipment.

And everyone can work to contain expenses and reduce the outflow of cash by cutting down on all waste. Get the most out of resources like computers. Find ways to get jobs done more efficiently so that less money is spent. If you can contribute to your company's cash and cash flow, you'll be valued.

DECIDING HOW AND WHEN TO USE CASH

We've outlined the ways in which a company can get and use cash, but knowing the options is a lot different from deciding what it *should* do. After paying its normal bills and operating expenses for running the business, the remaining cash flow can be used in a variety of ways (investment and financing activities), all with the goal of sustaining and growing the business.

A primary purpose of any business is to produce a *return* on the investment of its stockholders (owners or shareholders). And cash is just like any other asset: it should be used to produce a return. Consequently, two of the most important roles that business leaders play are

(1) determining how best to generate cash and (2) deciding how to use it wisely and efficiently to generate even more cash flow in the future.

Let's revisit Austin to see how a business owner or leader makes these kinds of decisions.

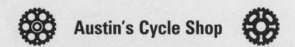

Austin's Cycle Shop

Austin had choices in what to do with the $25,000 cash he had at the end of his first year. He could put the entire $25,000 in the bank and have maximum liquidity. Or he could use part or all of it in investing activities, such as remodeling the building, making a down payment on a truck, or buying stocks or mutual funds for a greater return than his savings account offered. Or he could use it in financing activities, such as paying back part of his bank loan or repaying his investor.

But Austin decided that for maximum safety and liquidity, he would keep all of his $25,000 cash balance at the end of his first year in the bank. He had done well in the first year, but you never know when a competitor might open up across the street or a piece of equipment might break.

But in his second year, he had higher sales and more cash flow, so he decided to start using his cash. He paid back a portion of his bank loan, he bought a used truck so that he could offer to pick up and deliver customers' bikes, and he bought out his brother-in-law's investment. His brother-in-law was supposed to be a silent investor, but it didn't quite turn out that way and Austin was getting tired of the stream of advice he was getting during holiday meals.

Austin's Cycle Shop: Year 2 Cash from Operations			
Cash position end of year 1:			**$25,000**
Year 2: Total sales	**$100,000**		
Less: Operating expenses	(80,000)		
Cash flow from operations		$20,000	
Less: Pay back bank loan	(5,000)		
Pay used truck	(7,000)		
Pay back investor	(3,000)		
Total cash used in nonoperational activities		(15,000)	
Change in cash during year			+5,000
Cash position end of year 2:			**$30,000**

Austin could have used even *more* than $15,000 cash in nonoperational activities. He still had a cash position of $30,000. He could have used, say, $10,000 more ($25,000 total) to buy more equipment or pay off more of his loan. He would have ended the year with only $20,000 ($45,000 total cash available minus $25,000 used for investing and financing activities)—which is *less* cash than the $25,000 he had at the end of year 1.

Would ending the year with less cash than he started with have made Austin a bad manager? Not at all. He would have simply made a business decision that it was more important to his future operations to acquire assets, pay back the loan, and repay his investor. And because he generated more cash from operations—greater cash flow—in his second year ($20,000) than in his first ($15,000), Austin should be considered a good business manager, especially in a start-up enterprise.

Companies use cash generated from operating, investing, and financing activities for many good business purposes. The top uses of cash by corporations include paying dividends to stockholders, buying back stock, investing in mergers or acquisitions, investing in research and development (R&D), and making capital expenditures (investing in plants, equipment, real estate, etc.).

Obviously, having strong cash flow opens up more options for using cash to sustain and grow the business. Companies such as Apple, Google, and Microsoft, which generate lots of cash flow to create large cash balances, have massive capabilities denied to other companies with less liquidity. They can invest heavily in research and development, acquire other companies, pay to hire and develop top talent, and spend billions of dollars on marketing and advertising to generate more sales and more cash flow. They can take risks with new products, markets, and technologies—and fail—without a devastating impact upon their operations. And when they win, they win *big!* Apple, Google, and Microsoft are extremely profitable, in addition to being cash cows.

SO HOW MUCH CASH IS ENOUGH—OR TOO MUCH?

While a company can never have too much cash flow, its cash position is a little different. The rule of thumb for how much cash a company should keep on hand is: There is no rule of thumb about how much cash a company should keep on hand.

Every company differs in how much cash it needs for operations and to protect itself in case of a sudden financial hit (its reserves). CFOs, CEOs, and financial managers have to consider the following variables, among others, as they try to determine how much cash to keep tucked under the mattress, so to speak, and how much to reinvest in the company to keep it growing:

- The seasonality of the company's sales. If a company primarily sells year-end holiday decorations, it may need less cash in reserves in November and December (when it would have a lot of cash flow from sales) than in other months (when its cash flow is much lower).

- The company's growth trend and its forecast for future growth in sales.

- Strategic objectives that might require or generate a lot of cash, such as acquisitions, mergers, asset purchases, or product development.

- Estimates for cash reserves that might be necessary to address sudden changes in the industry or economy—the company's rainy day fund.

- The company's ability to borrow money or raise cash by selling stock. This is affected by the company's credit rating, current interest rates, debt levels, and how easy it is to access capital from lenders or investors.

- The average amount of time it takes to turn the company's investments, such as R&D, inventory, and receivables, into cash (the cash conversion cycle). For big retailers, it's not much time at all. For other companies, it can take awhile to sell through inventory or collect cash that's owed to the company.

Boeing, for example, began planning its newest plane, the 787, after the 9/11 attacks in 2001; it named the plane the "Dreamliner" in 2003 when it began serious development efforts. In 2007, it revealed its first prototype to the world at a launch party. After numerous delays, the 787 took its maiden flight in December of 2009. Boeing delivered the first 787 to customers in 2011, but with a backlog of more than 840 planes on order, it will be 2014 before some customers get their 787s. Once production is in full swing, the target is to assemble one airplane every three days—which sounds almost miraculous.

According to an article in the *Seattle Times*, "The company's original internal target for its own development costs was $5 billion. But . . . several Wall Street analysts estimate that fixing the litany of manufacturing problems, plus paying penalties to suppliers and airlines [for delays], has piled on an additional $12 billion to $18 billion" (Dominic Gates,

"Dreamliner's woes pile up," December 18, 2010). So what has Boeing done to appease investors? It has kept strong cash reserves. At the end of 2010, Boeing had $10.5 billion in cash and cash equivalents. Not a bad cash position, and one that keeps the company liquid and safe in the face of problems with getting a product to market.

Of course, companies can be criticized for holding cash. Can you imagine you or your family ever having too much cash? I'm sure it's a problem we would all like to wrestle with! A business, however, isn't exactly like a family. It *can* have too much cash, because its purpose is to produce a return on all assets, and cash sitting in a bank account isn't necessarily producing the best return possible.

Business leaders have to consider the following issues when looking at cash reserves:

- What is the rate of return on cash sitting in a bank account or mutual fund?

- What is the opportunity cost of hoarding large sums of cash rather than investing in new products, growing new markets, or making a strategic acquisition? In other words, what could have been earned by using the cash in an alternative investment?

If a company has too much cash, the leaders usually start looking for ways to reinvest it in the business. Stockholders may want the cash to be disbursed as dividends (a payment to investors for each share of stock they own) or used to buy back stock in order to reduce the number of shares outstanding (this would give existing shareholders a greater percentage of earnings per share owned, which may also mean an increase in the stock price).

Microsoft has been criticized for retaining too much cash, and shareholders have disagreed with management at times on how it should be used. In July 2004 it had over $70 billion in cash and liquid investments. Later that year it declared a special stockholder dividend of $32 billion, or $3.00 per share, possibly the largest total dividend in business history. With almost $40 billion in cash and investments today, Microsoft shareholders often question the need for so large an amount still held by the company.

While holding on to too much cash isn't necessarily a good thing, occasionally a company may choose to do it. Perhaps management has a strategy of conserving cash to prepare to make a major acquisition or to commit to a large-scale expansion. Or it believes the industry or general economy is headed for rough times and wants a sufficient reserve to ride out the storm. When the credit crisis began in December 2007, many companies reduced their expenditures in order to raise their cash balances. They were protecting themselves from the financial storm that could result from lower sales and limited access to capital through financing.

In 2006, Ford's new CEO, Alan Mulally, raised $23 billion by borrowing and leveraging assets. At the time, some questioned the strategy, but when the credit crisis caused what economists already call the "Great Recession", Ford was better positioned. While GM filed for bankruptcy and needed billions from the U.S. government to stay afloat, Ford was able to weather the storm.

Cash is fuel. Without it, the engine of a business can't run, the various moving parts can't function, and eventually the business slows down and dies. But for businesses flush with cash, the engine keeps revving faster and faster.

In the next chapter, we'll explore one of cash's closest counterparts—profit.

INSIGHTS INTO CASH

- Cash is the fuel of business. All companies require cash to operate, pay bills, and invest for the future. Lack of cash is a primary reason businesses fail.

- At any *point* in time, the cash position is the amount of cash on hand and in financial accounts, plus short-term securities convertible to cash within ninety days (called cash equivalents).

- During any *period* of time (month, quarter, year), cash flow is all cash collected from a company's operations (core business) *less* all cash used (disbursed) for expenses to run the core business. The ability to generate cash flow is usually considered more important than the amount of cash on hand at a given point in time.

- Liquidity refers to a company's available cash and its ability to turn its assets into cash quickly and inexpensively.

- A business gets and uses cash in three basic activities: (1) operations (core business); (2) investing, or buying and selling assets; or (3) financing, by receiving and paying back loans (debt) or selling stock to investors, paying dividends, or buying back its own stock.

- You can impact cash by helping to increase revenues, cut costs, delay (appropriately) payables (money owed by the company), and accelerate collection of accounts receivable (money owed to the company).

- A business with too much cash is earning very little return on this asset compared to what it might earn through alternative uses. Shareholders prefer that excess cash be invested or given back to them.

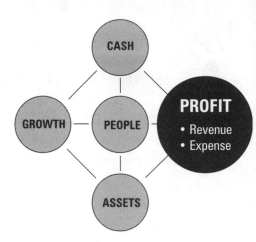

Chapter 2

PROFIT

Profit is like oxygen, food, water, and blood for the body;
they are not the point of life, but without them there is no life.
—*Jim Collins*

On March 10, 2000, the NASDAQ hit a high note, all because of trades for a special category of companies—the dot-coms. But then the slide began, and many of the companies that were traded in high volume and for amazing prices on March 10 no longer existed just a year or two later. Why?

No profits.

The dot-com bubble was an astounding time of speculation. Hundreds of companies went public even though they had never turned a profit. Everybody was sure that the future of e-commerce would push those numbers out of the red and into the black—but for many, it didn't happen. Quite simply, these companies couldn't generate enough revenue to cover their costs, either because of poor management or a poor market for their services. Warren Buffett famously avoided the dotcom crash because of his basic rule that if you don't understand how a company makes money, you shouldn't own the shares. He couldn't see a clear plan for profitability.

In the previous chapter, I said that cash is the fuel that drives the engine of any business. If that's true, then profit determines if and for how long that engine will keep running.

Profit is simply the difference between how much you make by selling goods and services (revenues) and how much it costs to produce and sell them (expenses), but it is not the same thing as cash flow, which I'll explain in a moment. Obviously, you want to sell your products for more than they cost! It's amazing how some businesses lose track of this simple idea. The dot-coms and all of their investors and stockholders epitomize the profit-blind behavior that can lead companies to their demise.

A company's future is ultimately determined by how much cash it generates from profits, where that cash comes from, and how rapidly and consistently it comes in over time. For publicly held companies, stock price is determined primarily by how quickly, by how much, and with what consistency investors believe the company will increase its profits. Just as with cash generation, your core business operations are the most important source of profits. Profit might also be earned from investments, selling assets, or other means. But your company's financial health is measured primarily by how profitably you can conduct your core business over time—to generate increasing sales, control expenses, and grow your income.

AKA

When discussing the profit for a company as a whole, people might use the terms *profit, net profit, income, net income, earnings,* or *net earnings.*

PROFIT AND CASH FLOW ARE DIFFERENT

While on the surface it might seem that profit and cash flow are just about the same, they are not. The differences amount to how each one is calculated and when each one is recorded on the books. These may seem like accounting technicalities, but each of these numbers is meaningful in a unique way, so it's important to understand the difference.

As we discussed in chapter 1, cash flow is the difference between actual cash received and actual cash used in the process of doing business (from core operations). Each day, month, quarter, and year, a company receives a certain amount of cash and pays out a certain amount of cash. It's that simple. Analysts look at cash flow carefully because it's a very real measure of how a company is doing (whether it will be able to pay its bills tomorrow or next week or next month).

Profit, on the other hand, is revenue from the sale of services and products—whether payment in the form of cash has been received yet or not—minus all expenses—expenses paid in cash, expenses to be paid in cash at a later date, and expenses accounted for in other ways.

While you could say that the profit isn't "real" because the cash hasn't moved in and out of the company, it's still important to know whether a company is earning income (making more than it's spending) from its daily operations over a period of time. If we didn't calculate profit (or income) this way, a company could appear to not earn any income one month, be hugely profitable the next, and so on, depending on when its bills are due and when its customers pay their debts. But that wouldn't be a very good indicator of how consistently it's earning income from its core operations, would it? Even if its financial performance was steady overall, it might seem erratic if we didn't follow this type of accounting system, which is called *accrual-basis accounting*.

Another way to think of accrual-basis accounting is that it tracks transactions. Sales, expenses, and profits are recorded when the transaction is made. Apple records the sale of a computer when the customer picks it up at the store and the expense for making the computer at the same time, even if the customer arranges to pay for it over several months and the cost of putting the computer together was paid a few months before the sale was ever made. Small companies may use cash-based accounting, in which you record a sale when cash is received and expenses when they are paid.

When we look at income statements in chapter 8, we'll explore all of the factors that affect the profit calculation.

THE BOTTOM LINE AND OTHER MEASURES OF PROFIT

When it comes to profit, there are two common measures people focus on: *gross profit* and *net profit*. Each of these measures is an important indicator of financial health.

Gross profit is a useful measure for companies on a day-to-day basis because it tells them how much money they are earning on each product or service they sell. Gross profit is calculated by subtracting the cost of a particular product or service (what it cost the company to buy or make it, or the *cost of goods sold*) from the sale price. More often, we refer to total gross profit, which is all revenue (sales from the core operations) less the total cost of goods sold. A company wants to earn as much as possible from each sale, so it will look at gross profit as it sets prices, decides whether to sell a product or service, determines the product and service mix it will offer, and decides how much money it should budget for buying or making a product or delivering a service.

When businesspeople talk about how profitable a company is, they are usually referring to the amount of net profit (net income) it earned. And when you hear leaders say that a new strategy is going to improve the bottom line, they are talking about net profit—because net profit is generally the last line, or the bottom line, on the income statement. Net profit is simply all revenue recorded by the company minus all expenses, including cost of goods or services sold, discussed above, and expenses not related to the sale of a particular good or service, such as salaries, rent, advertising costs, utilities, and so on. These costs are referred to as *operating expenses*, and I'll talk more about them later in the chapter. One operating expense frequently discussed is *overhead*, or *general and administrative costs*, which includes the salaries of support personnel, rent, supplies, and other similar items. Without a strong gross profit, a company can't book a net profit, because gross profit must be high enough to cover all of the operating costs.

For both gross profit and net profit, leaders and analysts will often focus on the profit margin, which is the amount of profit divided by the amount of revenue, expressed as a percentage. (The terms you'll hear them use are *gross profit margin* or *gross margin* or *net profit margin* or *net margin*.) Why do people care about margins? Because they tell us how efficiently a company is turning revenue into profit. For instance, if the net profit margin is 13 percent (the average for large companies), then thirteen cents out of every dollar received is profit. Even though one company has lower profit in dollars than another, its profit margin might be significantly higher, indicating a well-managed business that generates more profit from every dollar of revenue.

Note: You may see *gross margin* used interchangeably with *gross profit*. The two are not the same, but in casual usage, you may see gross margin with a dollar figure after it. When you do, what you are seeing is actually gross profit.

Let's return to the story of Austin and his bike shop to understand this better.

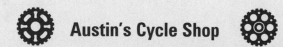

Austin's Cycle Shop

Austin has made it through year three of his business. He's a bit more established and feels confident that he can keep cash flowing to keep the doors open, but he's becoming more focused on profit. He needs to be if he wants to survive and grow. Austin's gross profit is his sales price per bicycle or part sold, less his direct costs of buying the bicycle or part from his supplier and any related costs. Austin's net profit will be what's left over from the gross profit of all his sales after he deducts his remaining operating costs: the salaries of the people working in the shop, rent for his shop space, advertising online and in local publications, utilities, interest on debt, and taxes.

For his third year of operations, this is what his profit looked like:

Revenue	140,000
Cost of goods sold (COGS)	(91,000)
Gross profit	49,000
Operating costs	(38,000)
Net profit before tax	11,000
Tax	(4,000)
Net profit (net income)	$ 7,000

Austin's gross margin is 35 percent ($49,000 / $140,000). His net margin is 5 percent (7,000 / 140,000). For retailers, those margins are average, but you'd expect higher than average margins for a specialty retailer like Austin.

The average net profit margin of the S&P 500 was about 13 percent in 2011. This means that for every one hundred dollars in revenue, a company would generate thirteen dollars in profits. Recall from the previous chapter that Microsoft generates substantial cash flow. It was also the fourth most profitable public company in the United States in 2010, earning $18.8 billion, and had a very healthy net profit margin of over 30 percent, well above the S&P average. Likewise, Apple and Coca-Cola beat the S&P average with net profit margins higher than 20 percent. Some would think that the two largest companies in America,

Walmart and ExxonMobil, would also enjoy a higher than average net profit margin, but they don't. ExxonMobil generated $30 billion in earnings in 2010, more than any other company that year; its net profit margin was 8.2 percent. Walmart generated $16.3 billion and had a net profit margin of only 3.8 percent, which means for every hundred dollars Walmart sells it generates three dollars and eighty cents in profits. These are all tremendously successful companies, so why the variation in their net profit margin?

Think about it this way: You don't have to buy your gas from ExxonMobil and you don't have to buy your milk from Walmart, but can you buy an iMac from someone other than Apple? Can you buy a license of Microsoft Office from someone other than Microsoft? While there are a lot of soda pop choices, my sister will order a water if Diet Coke isn't on the menu. Companies that sell commodities, products that are readily available from multiple vendors, will typically have lower profit margins compared to companies that are selling something unique or exclusive. Remember this: *If you're not unique, you better be cheap.*

TWO WAYS TO INCREASE PROFITS

Most company leaders would like to increase profits—and most investors would like companies to increase their profits. It is almost always a primary factor in a company strategy and can become the main focus, particularly if profits have been holding steady or declining. There are two fundamental ways to increase business profits from operations: grow revenues and/or reduce expenses. Strategies based on either of these goals can be difficult to execute and can have unexpected results. Sometimes growing revenues requires making investments that might not earn a return in the near future—or at all. Growing revenues by raising prices could have the effect of lowering sales. And reducing expenses requires careful analysis. If you cut employee benefits, for instance, you might lose valuable employees and incur greater costs to hire new people and train them. Many companies struggling during the recent downturn boosted their profits by laying people off. The challenge is that, as demand increases, they may not have enough of the right employees in place to meet their customers' needs.

Austin recognized the tricky situation he was facing.

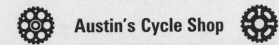

Austin's Cycle Shop

Austin was disappointed with his operations. His monthly sales revenue was increasing. However, his expenses had also been creeping upward. His cost of goods sold had suddenly jumped because of supplier consolidations and price increases. His overhead had also grown faster than sales because he had hired two part-time employees—a service and repair technician and a sales clerk.

Since Austin's margins were declining, he had a big problem: He wasn't earning much personally. If something didn't change, his family wasn't going to be able to afford his business much longer.

Austin was earning $300 for every higher-end bicycle he sold:

Product (bicycle) sales price:	$1,000
Cost of goods sold:	(700)
Gross profit:	$ 300

He had two options to increase profit: (1) raise revenues by increasing prices or selling more of his products and repair services, and/or (2) lower his costs. If he raised his prices, his gross profit would be greater on each bicycle sold, but he might sell fewer units and reduce his total gross profit. If he lowered his sales prices, he could sell more bikes, but at a lower gross profit. Would the increase in sales make up for that? If he could find some way to reduce his cost of goods sold (the cost of the bicycle), he could lower his price, maintain his gross profit on each unit, and increase sales, creating greater cash flow and profits. But the cost was set by his supplier.

The way Austin saw it, his two options were actually four:

A Try to negotiate with his supplier to lower his cost of goods sold to $600 to enable a lower sales price of $900 while keeping a gross profit of $300. The lower prices could increase sales, thus increasing total gross and net profits and cash flow.

B Try to lower cost of goods sold to $600, keep the same sales price of $1,000, and increase gross profit to $400.

C Increase the sales price to $1,100 if cost of goods sold stayed at $700, to generate higher gross profit of $400.

D Increase sales price to $1,100 and lower cost of goods sold to $600, to create gross profit of $500.

We'll find out what path Austin took in the following pages.

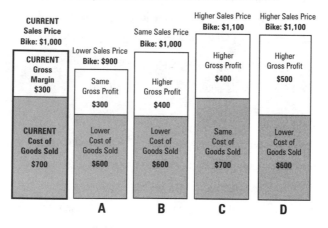

Relationship of Sales Price, COGS, and Gross Profit

Grow Sales Revenue

There are two ways to grow sales revenue: increase the price of the goods or services sold or increase the sales volume.

People might be willing to pay a higher price for your product (thus growing sales revenue and increasing gross profit) if there is value added to the product through enhanced features or better ongoing support, or if market demand supports the higher price. However, increasing the price might also result in fewer products sold; customers might not be willing to pay the higher price. The result could be *more* gross profit on each product sold, but *less* total gross and net profit.

Consider what happens when oil companies increase gas prices. When prices are in a steady upward trend, customers may buy more efficient vehicles, take fewer road trips, and ride the bus to work when they can. But using less gas requires changing our habits, sometimes substantially. The oil companies count on the fact that many of us won't be willing to make those changes. And for most of us, gas is a necessity; we won't stop buying it entirely unless we can no longer afford it.

If a company thinks it can't increase prices without hurting demand, it will often work to increase sales volume through strategies like the following:

- Lower prices to increase demand for the product.

- Innovate products and services to create new offerings that are more profitable or in higher demand.

- Improve the quality and skill sets of customer service and sales teams.

- Use aggressive marketing and sales strategies to drive demand for products. If you are in sales or marketing, your work will have a direct influence on generating more sales revenue.

- Open a new location, begin selling products online, or develop new distribution channels through relationships with other companies.

- Develop new customer markets through geographic or demographic diversification.

A new trend in the entertainment industry in the United States is helping concert promoters and artists ensure that tickets will sell—and maybe sell out—during tough economic times. Promoters are putting tickets on sale far in advance of the actual show, sometimes with a lead of almost a year. The goal is to get access to the limited dollars people have to spend on entertainment before somebody else does, such as a promoter of another show that same week or month. The promoters offering early purchase options are beating their competition to the market in order to meet their sales volume projections.

A classic example of increasing sales through price reduction is Henry Ford's plan to sell more cars by making them affordable to even his own factory workers. He presented his idea to his board, which, thinking that he was in the wrong, tried to oust him, even suing him for control of the company. But Ford prevailed. In 1909, prices were at $220. By 1914, he had slashed prices to $99. Margins on each unit plummeted, but sales skyrocketed, and net income rose from $3 million in 1909 to $25 million in 1914.

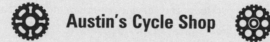

Austin's Cycle Shop

Austin decided customers would pay more for his products, so the first tactic he tried was to raise the price of his best-selling bike by $100. His gross profit per bike increased to $400. But instead of increasing his total gross profit, the strategy reduced his gross profit by $200! What happened? He had averaged ten sales per month for a total gross profit of $3,000—to be increased, he had hoped, to $4,000 (10 x $400). However, the next month he sold only seven bikes at the higher price for a total gross profit of only $2,800 (7 x $400). His strategy had backfired, so he dropped his price back to the original.

As Austin found out, if we increase our sales price too much, we can price ourselves out of the market. Customers will buy the same or similar products and services from our competitors for lower prices or because of perceived greater value—perhaps with added quality, warranties, services, or accessories for the same price.

If we keep prices the same, better advertising, better marketing, customer referral incentives, and broader distribution might drive increased sales. But these initiatives might require more costs to fund the additional marketing or distribution. And there is always the risk that sales won't increase enough to make up for the added cost. Keep in mind that for every unit sold, the cost of goods sold has to be accounted for, so the effect on the bottom line may be minimal.

Let's look at a simple example of the effect on the bottom line of increasing revenue. This company increased its revenue by $3,000, but notice the effect that has on net profit:

Increase in revenue	$ 3,000
Less: Cost of goods sold	(2,100)
Gross profit	$ 900
Less: Operating expense	(450)
(Due to higher marketing costs)	
Net profit before taxes	$ 450
Less: Taxes (33%)	(150)
Net profit	$ 300

Remember the law of profit margins. Only a small percentage (for most companies) of revenue produced turns into actual net profit. Here, $3,000 in additional revenue produced only $300 in net profit.

We're growing sales . . . and losing money! Many a business leader has heard this cry. It's not enough to grow sales revenue if you want to increase profit. If expenses are increasing at a faster rate than sales, you'll reduce profits until you lose money even though sales are going up! This is what happened to many of the dot-com businesses in the late nineties, which resulted in the dot-com crash at the turn of the century.

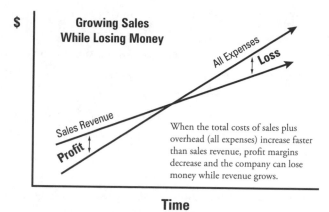

When the total costs of sales plus overhead (all expenses) increase faster than sales revenue, profit margins decrease and the company can lose money while revenue grows.

Like every business strategy, strategies for growing sales revenue have to be analyzed carefully.

Reduce Costs

Reducing costs to increase profit often seems like the easiest path, because reducing any type of expense (assuming the same sales volume) will result in increased profit for the company. There are many sources of costs in any business, so there may be lots of opportunities to make cuts without putting the burden on one particular area. However, the reality is that there are only so many costs that a company can control in the short term. For instance, short of abandoning a lease and paying all of the fines or fees for doing so, a company can't change the rent it pays on its properties until leases are up for renewal.

While cost cutting is often an easy target for any company trying to drive profit, it can't come at the expense of the customer. For example, in a cost-cutting move in 2007, Circuit City laid off all sales associates paid 51 cents or more per hour above an "established pay range"—essentially firing 3,400 of its top performers at once. Unfortunately, Circuit City found out too late that these higher-paid associates were the most knowledgeable about the products and in the best position to serve customers. Over the next eight months Circuit City's share price dropped by almost 70 percent and in November of 2008, the company declared bankruptcy.

Even so, companies need to constantly drive efficiencies and innovation to control costs and stay competitive. For any business, there are four basic categories of expenses or costs.

- Cost of goods sold (COGS)
- Operating expenses
- Interest expense
- Taxes

Cost of Goods Sold (COGS): COGS is sometimes called *cost of sales* or *direct cost* because it is directly associated with the production or sale of individual product units or services. These costs include the cost of raw materials and labor to manufacture products, the cost of inventoried products purchased from suppliers or distributors for sale in a retail business, and other similar expenses. COGS is sometimes called *variable costs* because the more products sold, the higher these total costs become; the total costs are reduced when sales volume declines. To be profitable, you must at least have a COGS that is less than your product sales price. As an accounting professor put it, "You can't lose money on the unit and make it up on the volume"—although some companies try hard to do it! If you are selling each unit at a loss, adding up a lot of negative numbers isn't going to give you a positive one. And to have an actual net profit, you must also have enough left over on every sale to cover operating expenses, interest, and taxes.

Many employees can influence the COGS by negotiating with suppliers, reducing scrap, and improving efficiency so less labor, cost, and time is needed. If you work in purchasing or procurement, you can focus on reducing the COGS by getting better prices on inventoried products or raw materials. But keep in mind that lowering COGS too much might result in lower-quality products or service—manufacturing defects, fewer upgrades or add-ons, or reduced customer service and support. Those lower costs might end up actually costing the company millions of dollars in lost sales revenue or recall expenses if quality suffers enough.

On the other hand, seemingly negligible cuts to cost can add up to a big boost for profits. To address its profit challenges, General Mills saved $1 million a year by reducing the number of pretzel shapes in its Hot 'n Spicy Chex Mix. It makes hundreds of such cost-cutting decisions each year through a process called margin management. By minutely analyzing every aspect of the product from ingredients to box size and the number of different varieties it offers, executives reduced the cost of goods sold for Hamburger Helper by 10 percent. And eliminating multicolored lids on Yoplait yogurt saved $2 million a year.

Operating Expenses: Operating expenses include salaries of support functions like IT, HR, and finance; travel; rent; utilities; sales and marketing expenses; research and development costs; and the cost of capital allocations for equipment and buildings used to run the business. Operating expenses that remain unchanged (over the short term) regardless of the volume of products sold are also called *fixed costs*. When a company goes through a period of lower sales and revenue, those fixed costs become very worrisome, and leaders have to start making tough decisions to sustain the company, such as laying off employees, hopefully with better results than Circuit City's. When times get really tough, they may implement mass layoffs, dismissing large numbers of people at once. In February 2011, as a result of the slow economic recovery, more than fourteen hundred companies had mass layoffs, involving a total of 130,818 people, according to the Bureau of Labor Statistics. And that was a good month compared to the previous two and a half years.

But in the absence of severe financial circumstances, companies often seek to lower their operating costs without ever considering laying off employees. And they turn to their employees to help them do it. Everyone within an organization can work to reduce overhead expenses by reducing waste of all types. If you're a manager, you might institute measures and metrics in key cost areas for your team to track, and then act on the data to improve efficiency. Human resources personnel can contribute by identifying the most effective and efficient people possible for positions at every level in the company. Leaders can make cost-cutting initiatives visible in the organization and communicate the reasons for them clearly.

Walmart, one of the world's largest companies (the largest in 2010), has strict cost controls throughout the organization. It searches for the most affordable healthcare options to offer its employees, and it combines shipments so that trucks drive with full loads, maximizing efficiency as it moves inventory throughout the country. Even Walmart's business executives fly coach.

Let's take a look at how Austin worked to reduce both his cost of goods sold and his operating expenses and see how that worked out for him.

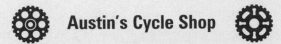 **Austin's Cycle Shop**

To lower his cost of goods sold, Austin began shopping for a new supplier who might compete for his business. It worked. He found a second supplier and used its pricing to negotiate a better deal with his current supplier. He was able to reduce his COGS by $100, putting his gross profit at $400. Sales held at about ten bikes per month, increasing his total gross profit to $4,000 per month. Things were looking up.

A few months went by with increasing sales, and Austin decided to take a risk and decrease his sales price to $950 to see if he could increase the number of bikes sold. Sales jumped up to twenty units each month and he was raking in $7,000 a month in gross profit. Things were going so well with the current price and gross profit that he decided to stick to the formula.

Austin was happy that his profits were on the rise, but he also realized that he could be doing a better job controlling his operating expenses—his overhead. For the year, his overhead would be higher than the previous year because he had two employees for the entire period. He was watching his bottom line carefully. New bike sales revenue was outstripping bike-servicing revenue, so he decided to reduce the hours of his service and repair technician. He also reduced the hourly pay of his sales clerk and created a sales commission incentive plan. His sales remained on an upward trend, and he felt sure his net profit margin would look better this year.

Interest and Other Expenses: Many companies, including Austin's, have other expenses that they have to account for, such as interest on loans, losses on investment transactions, or other expenses related to borrowing and investing money. Sometimes these expenses are one-time events (nonrecurring or extraordinary expenses) such as the purchase or sale of assets, a lawsuit, the discontinuation of a business unit, or other costs not associated with running the daily business. Companies will work hard to avoid some of these expenses (such as a loss on an investment), but expenses in this category are sometimes necessary if a company wants to make a bold move to grow, such as buying out a competitor.

Taxes: One factor that companies have to take into account as they work to increase profit is that they will also be increasing their taxable income, possibly increasing their federal, state, and local taxes. So cost-cutting measures don't result in a dollar-for-dollar increase in profit (just as revenue increases do not); the savings are partially offset by the increase in taxes due. But if a company reduces its tax liability directly, the money saved *does* increase its profit dollar for dollar.

How can a company do that? By reinvesting profits into the development of the business and taking advantage of tax breaks. General

Electric (GE) made the news in 2010 when it earned net income of $14.2 billion but, according to an April 16, 2010, CNN article, paid no U.S. federal taxes. A primary factor is that about $9 billion was earned overseas and reinvested. And GE's circumstances aren't unusual. Boeing paid no federal taxes from 2008 to 2010, Bank of America paid no taxes in 2010, and ExxonMobil paid no taxes in 2009, a year when it was the second most profitable company *in the world*. The tax code for businesses is complicated, and there are a variety of tax breaks that can reduce a company's taxable income to $0.

Many companies would rather use their money to invest in the company and grow it (expenses that reduce the bottom line) than pay taxes. So they may sacrifice profit in order to spend their money to further their overall strategy.

While reducing expenses can be difficult, it is often the most efficient way to improve the bottom line. Let's return to the example of increasing revenue. You'll remember that increasing revenue by $3,000 produced $300 in net profit. But what happens if we reduce the COGS for that revenue by $300 and operating expenses by $100?

Increasing Revenue by $3,000		Decreasing Expenses by $400	
Increase in revenue	$ 3,000	Revenue	$3,000
Less: Cost of goods sold	(2,100)	Less: Cost of goods sold	(1,800)
Gross profit	$ 900	Gross profit	$1,200
Less: Operating expense	(450)	Less: Operating expense	(350)
Net profit before taxes	$ 450	Net profit before taxes	$ 850
Less: Taxes (33%)	(150)	Less: Taxes (33%)	(280)
Net profit	$ 300	Net profit	$ 570

It took $3,000 in increased revenue to produce $300 in net profit. But it took only $400 in cost reductions to increase profit by $270. You can see why companies regularly institute organization-wide cost-cutting measures.

If a company wants to increase profits *and* continue to grow, it must increase revenues and control costs.

INSIGHTS INTO PROFIT

- Profit is the difference between the revenues you generate and the expenses incurred to create them.

- Profit is measured in dollars on the income statement and is also referred to as *earnings* or *income*.

- Gross profit is revenue less cost of goods sold. Net profit is revenue less all costs, including operating costs (overhead) and other costs. Profit margin (gross or net) is profit as a percentage of revenue (profit divided by revenue).

- Investors evaluate the worth of companies in large measure by their potential to consistently increase profits from their core business over time.

- Profits are increased by some combination of growing sales revenues and/or reducing costs.

- We can increase revenue by raising product prices and/or selling more products to the same or new customers.

- We can reduce costs by decreasing the cost of goods sold (direct costs) and/or reducing operating expenses (overhead or general and administrative expenses).

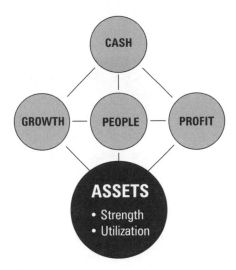

Chapter 3

ASSETS

Apple has some tremendous assets, but I believe without some attention,
the company could, could, could—
I'm searching for the right word—could, could die.
—Steve Jobs, on his return as interim CEO in 1997

Southwest Airlines is one of the largest domestic airlines in terms of the number of passengers who fly on its planes each year. And it has by far the best financial performance record in American commercial aviation. It has been profitable every year in its over-forty-five-year history, including the crisis period following 9/11. It was profitable even during the Great Recession that began in December 2007, while American Airlines, Delta, and United all lost billions of dollars. In 2010 Southwest earned $459 million in a still-tough economy.

How has it achieved such sustained profitability? A big factor has been smart, efficient use of its assets.

Its focus on fast turn times—time spent unloading and reloading planes—between flights, an average of twenty-five minutes compared to the industry average of thirty-five to sixty minutes, means that key assets like airplanes and pilots are idle for less time every day, month, and year.

Its strategy of point-to-point flights (rather than the traditional hub-and-spoke pattern of most major airlines) helps it minimize connection times, flight delays, total trip time, and fuel costs.

As a result, Southwest gains more flying time per pilot and requires fewer total employees per aircraft, using its human assets more efficiently.

Unlike other airlines that use a number of different types of aircraft, Southwest uses only one model: the efficient Boeing 737. Savings in crew training, maintenance and ground service personnel training and in parts and inventory, plus the capability to substitute any aircraft for any other, produce substantial efficiencies, cost savings, and passenger satisfaction.

Like Southwest's airplanes, fuel, hangars, and crews, everything a company uses to produce revenue is an asset. Whether tangible, like cash, buildings, or equipment, or intangible, like patents or copyrights, assets are the resources used to get the results leaders strive for. They support the financial strength of the company. Yet where assets are concerned, leaders face a dilemma—a dilemma at the root of many strategic decisions: how to balance asset *strength*, which provides flexibility in meeting obligations, taking advantage of opportunities, and surviving difficult economic conditions, with asset *utilization*, which generates a high return on investment to meet the stockholder objectives of sustained corporate growth and earnings.

WHAT ARE ASSETS AND HOW DO WE USE THEM?

Your house, your cash savings, your investments—these are all assets that you own. While you may not necessarily use them to produce revenue, you do use them to support a certain standard of living, to support your personal growth in a variety of ways.

Likewise, your company has assets and uses them to support its growth by producing revenue and profits. Without enough assets or the right combination of assets, your company can't remain in business; it can't be profitable. You sell your inventory of products (an asset) to generate revenue. You lease buildings to house your people and equipment to perform your work. You use transportation assets, like airplanes and trucks, for travel and shipping. You use cash assets (covered separately in chapter 1 because of their importance) to pay bills, to make investments, and to buy inventory, materials, and equipment. And your accounts receivable are assets that represent a source of future cash flow such as written contracts your company has with customers or other parties that indicate payments you will receive. Even your business relationships, such as joint ventures with other companies or a partnering agreement with a key supplier, can be considered assets, even if they are not listed on the balance sheet. They are used to produce revenue, cash flow, and profits for your business.

Intellectual property (IP) and patents can also be hugely important assets for some companies. In their book *Rembrandts in the Attic* (Harvard Business Press, 1999), Kevin Rivette and David Kline explain how Dow Chemical profited immensely from analyzing and maximizing the company's previously mismanaged IP assets. Forced to cut costs by an industry-wide recession in the early 1990s, Dow conducted a yearlong audit of its patents. The end result was $50 million saved immediately due to a reduction in taxes and maintenance fees for unneeded patents. But more important, better management of IP assets resulted in increased patent licensing revenues: They shot up from $25 million in 1994 to more than $125 million by the end of the decade.

Although they are not represented on any financial statement, your people (employees and customers) are your most important asset. Without them, none of your other assets make any money. Since employees and customers are central to a company's business success, they will be addressed in more detail in chapter 5.

ASSET STRENGTH: LIQUIDITY

How would you answer the question "How strong is your company?" You might think about your cash flow or your profit, but if you are speaking to a potential investor or analyst, they would also be interested in asset strength.

Your company's asset strength reflects its ability to meet its financial obligations now and in the future, to survive the storms and fluctuations of business, and to take advantage of profitable opportunities when they arise. It manages these feats of strength by possessing cash and other assets of greater value than its liabilities—its debts and future financial obligations. These assets and liabilities are communicated on the balance sheet, which we'll explore in chapter 9.

What is the most important indicator of asset strength? Liquidity. Recall from chapter 1 that the more liquid a business is, the more cash it has readily available (cash position), or can generate, quickly and without much cost, for important purposes: solving difficult problems, riding out down markets, and creating or taking advantage of opportunities to grow. And businesspeople can make an important impact on a company's liquidity by conserving cash and contributing to cash flow. Cash, and the ability to generate cash, is perhaps your company's most important asset—after its people.

Anything that impacts cash positively (see chapter 1) strengthens your assets. Increasing product prices, decreasing costs, selling more products, or introducing more products can all improve your company's cash position and strengthen your asset base and liquidity. With more cash, the company can acquire many different types of assets—including other businesses—to make more money.

Because liquidity or asset strength is so important, we examine it from multiple angles. Leaders look at the total value of assets and subtract the total amount of liabilities (financial obligations like debt) to see what's left over (hopefully a positive number). This is called equity, and just like the equity in your home (its market value minus what you owe on your mortgage), it represents a reserve for possibly raising cash. Analysts might also look at equity as part of a ratio comparing it to total debt (called the debt-to-equity ratio). We'll discuss these measures in more detail in chapter 9.

Leaders and accountants are also concerned with a company's ability to cover its debts in the short term, so they compare cash and other liquid assets to bills that have to be paid in the next twelve months (called short-term liabilities). Stronger companies can pay their bills and still have liquid assets left over. If you have just enough liquid assets on hand to cover yourself for twelve months, your asset strength may be shaky. If your revenue suddenly drops, or a customer delays paying you, you may have trouble making payments. And if a compelling opportunity for growth suddenly crops up, you may not be able to take advantage of it. However, some strong companies, such as Walmart, have lower levels of liquid assets in relationship to short-term liabilities but generate such massive and steady cash flow that there is no concern about the company's ability to meet its obligations.

Finally, the nature of your company's assets, particularly assets used to generate revenue versus those that aren't, influences asset strength. For example, large amounts of real estate or other fixed assets not used to produce revenue provide less financial strength than the same dollar value in assets that are directly used in producing revenue.

Credit rating agencies such as Standard & Poor's (S&P) and Moody's use this information about asset strength, plus in-depth analysis of financial history, profit and cash flow generation, and other information, to assess the risk to investors of lending money to, or purchasing stock in, companies. The more equity a company has, the less risky it is, because it has resources to fall back on in case of troubled times. But rating agencies don't only assess companies. S&P made headlines in August of 2011 when it downgraded the United States from its AAA credit rating (for the bonds it sells to raise money) for the first time in history.

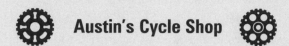

Austin's Cycle Shop

Austin, as always, was searching for ways to grow his business and become more profitable. He saw his larger competitors in the market thriving as the popularity of cycling as a form of exercise and as a competitive sport grew. He wanted to take advantage of the boom, but was struggling. Austin had been digging into his cash over time, and now he had an opportunity that could change his future profits, but he wasn't sure he could take advantage it.

Austin's supplier said that if he placed larger orders for bicycles, parts, and accessories (his inventory, an asset), he could get a substantial discount. If he could reduce his cost of goods sold, Austin could lower his sales prices—which could mean more units sold and more profit.

But Austin would need more up-front cash and storage space, which he didn't have. He couldn't sell his inventory of bicycles and parts faster to generate more cash flow because he didn't want to lower his prices any more. He could not borrow any more money because the bank didn't think he had enough asset strength to support a loan: His liquid assets were not sufficiently large in relationship to his liabilities.

Austin wondered if he had been neglecting his asset strength and if it would cost him a major opportunity to take his business to the next level.

He started thinking about bringing in an equity partner to invest in the shop. With more cash, his balance sheet would be stronger, his liquidity would improve, and he would be able to place larger inventory orders, lower his price, sell more bikes faster, and generate more cash and profit.

It was the best choice, he decided, and he started the process of seeking out an investor.

Liquidity is an important aspect of asset strength. However, cash doesn't earn a great return, which brings us back to the dilemma mentioned at the beginning of the chapter: balancing liquidity with utilization.

ASSET UTILIZATION: PRODUCTIVITY

Accumulating assets, particularly liquid assets, can be a necessary strategy for some companies, but the purpose of assets, even cash, isn't to be socked away. The purpose of assets is to be put to use to generate revenue, a return on the asset. However, while cash doesn't earn a very high return, utilizing cash to acquire other assets that earn higher returns can mean less flexibility in meeting unforeseen problems or opportunities, which typically require ready cash.

When leaders discuss asset utilization, they mean how effectively and efficiently you use your assets to produce revenue or to reduce costs. The biggest factor in asset utilization is productivity: the amount of work accomplished or goods produced per unit of assets used (including equipment, time, labor, people, or cash).

A machine making one hundred widgets per day is more productive, and is being better utilized, than a similar widget machine making only fifty per day. This is a case of underutilization of an asset. In your company, you can play a role in identifying, reducing, or eliminating underperforming assets and replacing them with more efficient ones. And you can look for ways to use existing assets more efficiently.

Stretch your mind a little as you look for creative ways to maximize asset productivity. Kingsford, the leading manufacturer of charcoal in the United States, was founded when Henry Ford learned of a way to turn the wood scraps from automobile production into charcoal briquettes. Ford in effect converted the waste from one asset into an asset in its own right!

Measuring productivity is almost a science. There are many different types of assets, and you need different types of measures to determine how productive each asset is. For instance, how you measure the productivity of a marketing employee is substantially different from how you measure the productivity of a widget machine. While there are some universal financial measures, many companies (think about manufacturing companies) need to understand in fine detail how productive each asset is to make sure they are investing wisely and using each asset to maximize the return on those investments.

Let's begin by looking at employee productivity. The productivity of employees reflects how much work employees can accomplish (as measured by tasks accomplished or work product created) in an hour, day, week, etc. For example, a call center employee properly handling twelve calls per hour is more productive than one handling only eight calls per hour with the same degree of effectiveness. However, if we have to pay the higher-performing employee twice as much to produce 50 percent more than the lesser-performing employee, the company might not be better off. And the key phrase is "properly handling calls." If the more productive employee is rushing through calls, leaving customers dissatisfied, then the employee isn't actually more productive in the big picture.

A company has various ways to determine the productivity of its workforce, depending upon the nature of its business, industry, and the specific functions individual workers perform. One measure is how much revenue is produced, or the total dollar value of goods or services sold, divided by the total number of employees. In some companies, all employees have to track their time to projects they work on. This is particularly true in service companies, such as law firms, advertising agencies, accounting firms, and design firms, which need to be sure they are being paid for the assets they utilized in performing the work. The clients are billed for every hour worked by any employee on their projects. But in recent years, law firms in particular have been condemned for overbilling—inflating the hours listed on invoices. And in Florida, the top officials of a security firm were actually arrested on racketeering charges as a result of defrauding one county by millions of dollars. According to whistleblowers, the company sometimes left security posts empty because it didn't have enough staff (assets) to fill them, but billed the county for the time worked anyway.

At work, do you ever think, "It takes too long to get things done around here"? Do you work in any system or process that can be improved? One way to assess how efficiently assets are being used to achieve certain goals, such as completing a project, making a sale, or creating a product, is to measure *cycle time*. Cycle time is the total time required to complete any activity or process, and includes the time taken between initially thinking up a "big product idea" and actually getting it to market; between receiving an insurance claim and processing it; between receiving raw material and manufacturing a finished product and shipping it; or between deciding to hire a new employee and having that new employee report to work on his or her first day.

Whenever the cycle time of a business process can be reduced, productivity is increased, time is saved for other uses, costs are saved, and people and other assets are better utilized. This is often called business process improvement. McDonald's is known as *the* innovator in standardized, efficient processes that have become fast-food industry norms. Anywhere you go in the world, you will find that a Big Mac and the process for making it and serving it are virtually the same. Business process improvement is a key factor in helping people and other assets perform more productively. You can work with your team and others in your company to identify and streamline your processes, particularly the process of making and implementing decisions, which eats up a lot of time in some companies.

Inventory is also an asset, and a particularly important one for retailers. The productivity or utilization of inventory is measured by *inventory turnover*, or the number of times a company sells through its average inventory in a year. If a retail shoe store such as Payless carries, on average, inventory worth $100,000 in retail sales value, and if its annual sales are $1 million, then it sells out its inventory an average of ten times per year for an inventory turnover of 10. If a competitor has a similar shoe inventory worth $100,000, but has an inventory turnover of 20, then the competitor sells twice the volume and makes twice the revenue ($2 million) and twice the total gross profit. Note that inventory turnover can also be calculated as cost of goods sold divided by inventory.

While determining the productivity of individual assets is important in making day-to-day management decisions, broader strategic decisions—whether to take on more debt, whether to improve cash position, etc.—may be affected by your company's overall asset utilization. Asset utilization is measured by *return on assets*, which is your profit divided by your total assets (reported on your balance sheet).

These measures are some of the tools leaders use to make tough decisions in how they balance asset strength and asset utilization.

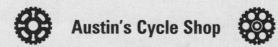

Austin's Cycle Shop

Austin only wanted to work with an investor who was knowledgeable about his industry and who could bring experience to the table. He'd tried the silent investor path with his brother-in-law, and that hadn't worked well. As he talked to investors and as they looked at his financial statements, they asked questions about his operations, specifically how he was utilizing his assets. When Austin began considering their questions, he came to some important realizations about his company.

First, he was not using his human capital in the smartest way possible. He had his one sales associate, who worked for part salary and part commission, working hours when Austin couldn't or didn't want to be in the store, which really meant when business was slow. But now he realized that he also needed her there when business was booming, to help close more sales. So he decided to shift her hours so that she could generate more sales per hour of work.

He was also wasting leased space. He was storing a fair amount of inventory in the back room, when he could be using the space to expand his bike service and repair operation. His was one of the few shops that offered that service, so he needed to maximize it. He could lease warehouse space for much less than his retail space, and then use his retail space to generate more service revenue. He would have to hire another technician, but his margin on service was better than his margin on bike sales, so he thought it would be worth it.

Making these two simple changes in how he utilized his assets resulted in immediate growth in sales and profit. And the interest of two investors.

ASSET STRENGTH VERSUS ASSET UTILIZATION: MAKING THE TOUGH DECISIONS

Let's say you inherit $100,000 in cash. What can you do to be financially secure and also earn more income? You could put it all in a money market fund for 1 percent or less today and have maximum liquidity and financial strength. Or you might use all the cash to buy a condo or townhouse outright—no mortgage or monthly payments. You can rent it out, have very low costs, and have a healthy 10 to 12 percent return. You would have higher utilization, but no cash left over, little financial strength, and no liquidity.

However, there is a third option, one that is more balanced. You could balance your need for both strength (liquidity) and utilization (return) by putting $50,000 into a money market fund and using the remaining $50,000 as a 50 percent down payment to buy a $100,000 property. Although you would have a mortgage payment, you would still receive a good return on renting the property, plus the modest return from the $50,000 in the money market fund. Voilà! You have both asset strength and utilization.

Similarly, a business needs to balance the amount of low-yielding cash it retains for liquidity with the need to put its cash to work by investing in higher-yielding but illiquid assets. A company can buy additional business units, invest in production plants, purchase capital equipment, and borrow at a lower interest rate to invest the proceeds at a higher yield to increase utilization. But in that scenario the financial strength (liquidity and ratio of debt to assets) of the company is reduced, so investment opportunities need to be balanced with the need for liquidity.

Maximum STRENGTH	Maximum UTILIZATION
• All cash position, maximum liquidity—minimum investment in other assets, such as buildings, equipment, plants, inventories, or other businesses	• Low cash and cash equivalents—because cash earns minimum current return
• Little or no debt	• High debt compared to equity
• Excellent strength to meet obligations and overcome difficulties	• Assets are mostly inventories, fixed assets, and business units that earn high returns
• Very little current return on cash assets, minimum to no investment for future return or company growth	• Maximum income-producing assets and greater debt fuel growth, but result in less ability to overcome problems and meet new opportunities that require cash

To find this balance, every businessperson involved in these types of decisions must understand how to assess the return on investment expected when using cash or loans to get access to an asset.

Analyzing Opportunities for Balance: Return on Investment

Everything in business requires *decisions*.

And many decisions ultimately require spending money, or investing capital. How do businesspeople determine whether to spend money to acquire a particular asset? The better decision is frequently the one that provides a greater return on investment (ROI) than the alternatives being considered. Determining ROI for individual project choices can help obtain balance.

Any investment in assets (buildings, manufacturing plants, large equipment, machinery, vehicles, etc.) should produce some sort of income stream or contribute to the production of revenue. At a minimum it must generate a return greater than the interest paid on the loan to buy the assets (or the interest that could have been earned on the cash). Typically, the income or profit produced by any asset divided by its cost is the ROI for that asset. However, ROI can be measured in many ways: retail sales organizations, for example, might measure annual sales per square foot of their retail stores. Ultimately, calculating ROI comes down to *cost-benefit analysis*. To do this type of analysis, first determine the costs of the opportunity or investment (cost) to be made (cash, labor costs, the cost of running a machine, etc.), and then assess the *benefits* to be gained (how revenue or product value could be created). Then, divide the benefit by the cost to calculate the percentage return on the investment.

$$\frac{\text{Return, or Benefit}}{\text{Investment, or Cost}} = \% \text{ ROI}$$

Identifying the benefits of alternative options through ROI analysis is an extremely important application of business acumen. This analysis helps you compare "apples with apples" when considering very different opportunities.

Walmart, for example, uses ROI analysis when determining where to open new stores. If it is considering two or three locations, it will first estimate how much profit it expects to generate from the new store. It will then look at the cost of leasing space (or building its own building) in the different locations. While it might seem easy to just divide the anticipated annual profit by the annual cost of the lease to determine

ROI, there are other factors to consider. For instance, one location may have better traffic patterns, which could result in increased sales and profit. While the lease in that location might be more expensive, the resulting profit might be worth it. Another factor is the community response. If the community is resistant to Walmart opening in the location that has better traffic flow, that could potentially hurt sales. All of these factors and more have to be assessed carefully when determining how to use cash to invest in a lease for a new store.

ROI analysis also includes risk assessment. In general, riskier investments should require the opportunity to receive a higher return than safer investments. The potential of higher return compensates for taking the greater risk. If one opportunity is relatively safe and can yield a 12 percent ROI, and the alternative is highly risky but will yield only 15 percent, then the 12 percent option could be the better choice. The increased risk may not be worth just a little more return. You might consider a riskier asset investment more seriously if the possible ROI is 50 percent or 80 percent or 200 percent.

If you're in a position to buy assets, make recommendations to purchase office equipment, real estate, or technology, make other capital investments, or hire people, always evaluate the ROI. To learn more about different measures of or factors in ROI, go to our website, www. seeingthebigpicture.com.

If assets are not producing good returns, they should be sold to increase cash reserves or invested in other assets that will generate greater profits and cash flow. Many companies sell fixed assets, such as land and buildings, to invest the money in income-producing assets, such as new product lines or productive equipment. Some companies sell their office buildings and lease them back—the return they can get on the cash freed up is greater than the cost of their lease. In January of 2011, GE completed the sale of its majority stake in NBCUniversal, took the $8 billion, and put it to work buying energy companies that have a higher long-term growth potential and greater competitive advantage.

Opportunities and Vision Drive Asset Decisions

Of course, all of the analysis in the world doesn't matter if a company isn't keeping an eye out for opportunities to produce a greater return on its assets and to use those assets to grow. Some of the greatest companies in the world are great because they chose to reach beyond their competitors and invest in assets (often through research and development) that would help them grow in the future—help them access new markets, help them create unimagined products, help them solve a problem never solved before.

FedEx invented the overnight package delivery industry as we know it today. It developed technological assets to innovate package-tracking capabilities. It also innovated the use of other assets (planes, personnel, physical facilities) to grow quickly and profitably worldwide, although UPS, its largest domestic competitor, controls a larger percentage of the market. In its 2010 fiscal year, FedEx had revenue of almost $35 billion and realized over $1.18 billion in net income (profit). Its capital expenditures for the year were $2.8 billion, of which $1.5 billion was investments in more fuel-efficient aircraft. Yet its annual return on assets was substantially lower than UPS, a company that already puts a lot of time and effort into using its assets efficiently (going so far as to develop routes that contain as few left turns as possible, saving fuel and the driver's time). Will FedEx's investments into more efficient assets pay off in the future with continued growth in market share and profit? We'll see.

Some companies come out ahead by wisely opting out of certain assets and opportunities. JPMorgan Chase reported profits in 2008 when other investment banks were closing or suffering huge losses. It has largely avoided the investment in assets that poisoned so many financial institutions: mortgage-backed securities. As a result, it was able to acquire the troubled firms of Bear Stearns and Washington Mutual on favorable terms, recognizing that these assets could be used for significant future benefit under better management.

Where is your business, your market, the economy headed? Forecasting accurately and assessing those future changes with the vision of your company as a guide will help you plan your asset needs more effectively. Consider inventory levels, staffing requirements, customer service personnel, raw material needs, and any other significant asset demands of your business based on your plan for the future. If you can forecast accurately, making adjustments now can save or make money in the future.

INSIGHTS INTO ASSETS

- Assets include anything of value, tangible or intangible, used to produce revenue and profit or that can be converted to cash. Although they aren't listed on the balance sheet, people (your employees and customers) are considered by many to be a company's most important asset.

- Leaders face the constant challenge of balancing asset strength and asset utilization to produce the maximum return on investment and to ensure growth and profitability.

- Asset strength or financial strength is measured by the amount and nature (liquid or illiquid, productive or nonproductive) of your assets. Asset strength affects the overall capability of your company to pay its bills, meet its financial obligations, overcome difficulties, take advantage of opportunities, and generate cash flow and profits.

- *Liquidity* refers to how easily and rapidly your assets can be turned into cash. More liquid companies have greater capability to move quickly to solve problems and take advantage of market opportunities.

- Employees can impact asset strength by doing anything that benefits cash position.

- Asset utilization is the measure of how productively your assets are working to make money—to drive sales and profits.

- The productivity of employees reflects how much work employees can accomplish and is often affected by the tools and technology they have and the training and education they receive.

- Inventory turnover measures how many times a year you sell through your average inventory.

- Return on assets is a measure of how efficiently and productively a company uses its assets.

- Employees can improve asset utilization by eliminating inefficient or nonproducing assets, getting more productivity from existing assets, making business processes more efficient, and by working to use personal time more effectively.

- Leaders work to balance asset strength and utilization by carefully assessing all opportunities, particularly using return on investment and similar forms of cost-benefit analysis. The vision and forecast for the company, the industry, and the overall economy also affect asset decisions.

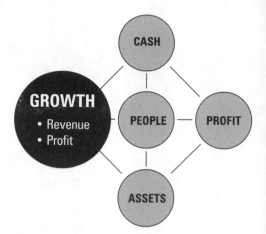

Chapter 4

GROWTH

You should approach growth not as an assumption,
but as a well-thought-out decision.
—Edward D. Hess

The dot-com industry has had a fairly checkered past in terms of the viability and survival of businesses. But unlike so many dot-coms, Amazon has not simply survived—it has thrived. Jeff Bezos launched his operations in 1995, and if you had wanted to buy all the outstanding stock of Amazon in December 2011, it would have cost you about $90 billion.

The growth lesson from Amazon is that Bezos made a deliberate, strategic decision to constantly reinvest cash in the business to push growth. In its first full year of operations (1996), Amazon.com generated $15.7 million in sales. Revenue was eight times that the following year. By the end of 1999, sales were $1.6 billion. Yet the company wasn't profitable until 2003.

In the early years of Amazon's life cycle, venture capital was available, Bezos assembled an able management team, and market conditions were right. Then in 1997, the company went public. However, by

2000, in the midst of the dot-com bust and without profits to back up its worth, the company's stock had lost two-thirds of its value. Strategic changes were made in management's planning and execution, including the very nature of the company they were building.

Eventually, Bezos's strategy to "get big fast" by gaining market share, building brand equity, and worrying about profits later paid off. After booking its first profit in 2003, the numbers skyrocketed. In 2007, profits were $190 million, and in 2010 Amazon produced profits of $1.152 billion and generated $3.495 billion in cash from its operations.

The phrase "grow or die" reflects the realities of the business world. If your company does not grow—expanding product and service lines, cultivating new customers and markets, increasing its financial strength and ability to attract new capital for further growth—your competitors will. They will draw away your customers and erode your market share, and that will set the company on a downward spiral that can be hard to escape. Not every business needs to grow at the level of Amazon, but without growth, most businesses can't survive. But why is that?

Constant change is a reality in today's business environment, and growth is one of the only ways to handle it. Change forces a company to adapt to new competition, to anticipate evolving customer needs, and to look for new opportunities—it forces a company to grow. Companies that merely seek status quo will see change as threatening, while companies with a growth mind-set will look for the opportunities that change can bring.

Investors expect growth, employees are energized by it, customers are attracted to it, and executives are measured by it.

WHY FOCUS ON GROWTH?

Have you ever worked for a successful, profitable, high-growth company? What was it like? Exciting, I bet. People were energized. They saw new opportunities to be involved in interesting projects. Career paths opened up as the company expanded its operations, products, and markets. Talented people joined the organization, offering stimulating perspectives and innovative ideas. Productivity increased, bonuses were handed out, and salaries were competitive. Morale was high. I imagine that's what it's been like for many employees of Amazon over the years.

But for companies that aren't growing, the picture is very different. If a company isn't adapting to changes in its environment by offering greater value, better prices, or innovative products, customers turn to aggressive competitors, the company begins losing market share, and the best people leave. Sales stall and then decrease; margins and profitability shrink; stock price drops and shareholders are disappointed; cost-cutting increases; people are let go; morale decreases; productivity, quality, and service fall; more customers turn to competitors and the company loses more market share; stock price drops further; sales decrease even more; profitability shrinks further . . .

Well, you get the sad picture.

These vastly different pictures explain why growth may be your CEO's number-one priority. And long-term, sustainable, profitable growth is the primary objective of any CEO of a publicly held company—who wants to keep his or her job! There may be small mom-and-pop operations that continue year after year at about the same level of sales and profitability. But any larger or publicly held enterprise that does not grow its sales and profits risks this "downward decline and die" cycle that ultimately spells doom, or at least a buy-out by a competitor. In the technology sector, lack of foresight and growth can lead to particularly swift failures and buyouts. In 2010 HP jumped into the tablet and smartphone market by rescuing Palm Inc., which hadn't been able to keep pace with surging competitors like Apple, Google, and Samsung. HP struggled to grow their new division and less than a year later, in the summer of 2011, it announced plans to terminate their tablet and smartphone initiatives.

If your company is publicly held, your CEO is focused on growth because people buy stock hoping that the share price will rise and/or dividends will be paid. The stockholders elect the board of directors to oversee their investment. And the board hires the CEO to successfully run the company—to assure that the stock price goes up. The CEO can't control the price of your company's stock in the investment market. However, the surest way any CEO can influence company stock price is to build a "growth company"—to increase sales revenue and profit year after year.

But how do we measure growth?

AKA

When businesspeople talk about a company's growth, they are usually referring to the growth of its revenue, but may also be referring to the growth of its income or profit.

GROWTH IN THE TOP LINE AND BOTTOM LINE

A company measures its growth in many ways: increase in number of employees, market share, number of offices, number of states or countries served, number of customers, amount of assets, and so on.

But when we speak of a company's growth, we are usually referring to its top-line revenue growth and bottom-line profit growth. *Top line* refers to the first line on the income statement: revenue. By what percentage did company revenues grow this year compared to last? Or how much did they grow in one quarter this year compared to the same quarter last year?

As we discussed in chapter 2, the *bottom line* is a company's net income or profit, shown on the last line of the income statement. The increase in percentage, or the *rate* of growth of both revenue and profit, is a widely used criterion for evaluating the worth, and stock price, of any company. However, a business can grow its top-line revenue but have its bottom-line profit decline. How is that possible? Because its costs increase at a faster rate than its increase in sales.

While it might seem obvious that a company should grow its sales faster than its costs, this isn't always easy to do. Companies striving to grow have to take risks and make decisions about investments in the future. If they misjudge a future growth opportunity, or if competitors undercut their prices and steal customers, or if the economy takes an unexpected downturn, companies can find their costs increasing faster than sales. And some growth strategies require leaders to reinvest potential profits into the company again and again. As we saw earlier, Amazon followed that strategy for years.

For many companies, declining profits or lack of profits in the short term may not be an issue. But over time, the bottom line is more important than revenue growth, a lesson learned by all of the dot-coms that didn't make it through the crash of 2001.

Wall Street looks closely at growth in earnings or profit and at earnings per share (EPS) as critical measures of growth, especially for a mature company. They've realized that if a company's total costs continually exceed its total revenue, it will ultimately be unable to borrow or raise other capital to finance its deficit. Eventually, a company with a shrinking bottom-line—regardless of top-line growth—will be forced to file for bankruptcy or just go out of business.

ORGANIC AND INORGANIC GROWTH

Companies grow revenues and profits in two ways: *organically* (internal growth) or *inorganically* (growth through mergers or acquisitions). Some businesses adopt one approach over another, while others use a combination of the two. Neither model is right or wrong; both have benefits and drawbacks.

A business grows organically, or from the inside, when it hires and trains new employees, opens new offices or stores, builds new plants to produce more goods or to serve different customers, expands its marketing initiatives and product sales into new areas geographically or demographically, or introduces new products and services developed by its workforce.

Organic growth offers maximum control over the timing of the expansion and the nature of the operations. There is generally less risk because management controls most aspects of the endeavor, and the company is usually expanding into business arenas it already understands.

And every person in a company can contribute to organic growth by helping to increase sales revenue and profitability. Functions such as sales, marketing, product or brand management, strategic planning, or retail store management have a direct influence. But support functions like human resources, IT, and finance also contribute to growth. For example, people in human resources can become more effective in the timely, prioritized hiring of talented employees to increase sales, build customer loyalty, and manage the organization more efficiently, resulting in reduced costs and increased margins.

With organic growth, however, the business also incurs 100 percent of the costs of expansion and operation, which can be considerable. The management team must stay on top of all aspects of the new offices, stores, or plants and oversee the hiring and training of all the new people—none of which is particularly easy! Organic growth can also be slow; it takes time for new sales territories to generate revenue, for new people to become fully trained and productive, and for new plants to become profitable.

So to grow revenue more rapidly, many companies buy, or merge with, existing businesses. This inorganic growth is faster than organic growth because existing customers and revenue streams are immediately acquired. Management teams, employees, production plants, offices, salespeople, and other company assets are already in place. Product brands and distribution channels are already established.

In 2010, sales were strong for both Apple (up 52 percent) and

Google (24 percent); because sales of their products and services were up, they were experiencing strong organic growth. However, Microsoft had sales up only 6.9 percent in 2010, after dropping 3.3 percent in the previous year. Investors saw that the company was not experiencing strong organic growth, and Microsoft's stock price trailed behind Apple's and Google's. That's one of the reasons why Microsoft resorted to a big purchase—paying 40 percent more for Skype than what many analysts thought the company was worth.

But inorganic growth carries its own set of challenges. It takes substantial capital to acquire another business. And the objective of reducing costs by combining operations is rarely carried out seamlessly: Employees might be terminated, undermining morale and productivity; information and technology systems might be incompatible, requiring more cash investment and causing delays; and merging organizational cultures can raise unanticipated resistance. In fact, various studies have shown that about 70 percent of all mergers and acquisitions don't meet the business objectives set by the senior leadership team. While some work out wonderfully, like the match between Disney and Pixar, others actually erode the value of the business. After Sprint and Nextel merged in 2005, Nextel experienced an exodus of executives and managers, most citing incompatible cultures within the two freshly partnered companies. From there, it just got worse—fierce competition and a bad economy forced Sprint/Nextel to lay off many workers, and stock prices dropped dramatically.

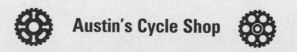

Austin's Cycle Shop

Austin was in his seventh year now. His margins were strong, he was profitable, and he was making a nice living from the business. But Austin was ambitious, and he knew there were market opportunities to be pursued.

The city he was in had grown geographically over the previous six years. One newer residential neighborhood didn't have a bike shop yet, and he wanted to beat his competitors into it. He had already scouted out some space that would work well for his needs and that had good foot traffic. Opening another shop would also make him the first local bike shop to have more than one location.

At the same time, he found an opportunity to buy another store near campus from an owner who was ready to retire. With more stores, Austin could buy inventory for all the shops at greater discounts, tap into the college market, and drive more cash and profit. Motorized scooters had become popular among students, and adding this product line in the acquired store could increase sales. Austin also knew that if he didn't buy the shop, another competitor might, buying market share and potentially cutting into his business.

Could he do both moves at once? Acquire a competitor and open a shop in a new neighborhood? Although he'd heard horror stories about acquisitions, he thought that in this case, opening a new store in an untested market was possibly the riskier growth strategy.

Austin has asset strength, and he thought he could get enough capital from his investor and the bank. But to analyze the return on these investments (ROI), he decided to develop a business plan for his company's future expansion. He had to figure out how much cash he would need, carefully assess projected revenue and profit from the new stores, analyze personnel needs, explore lease costs in the new neighborhood, and gather a host of other information about costs and opportunities to present to investors. He just hoped they saw the potential he saw.

GROWTH AND THE BUSINESS LIFE CYCLE

Start-up, growth, maturity, decline: These are the classic stages of a business's life, although management gurus of various stripes and colors have put their own spin on the idea of the business life cycle. While this is a useful way to think about how a company develops and grows, it's also misleading, because having one stage labeled "growth" implies that the company isn't growing the rest of the time. Of course it is—until it's declining. And while we use the term *life cycle*, businesses rarely progress from one stage to another in a step-by-step fashion. A company might move back and forth between growth and maturity as new markets or technologies become available. Or a new division within a mature company might exhibit all of the behaviors of a start-up.

Still, the growth of a company changes over time, and using the stages of the life cycle helps us anticipate what type of growth we might expect in a company. For instance, a start-up might struggle along for a while with little growth, just enough to keep it alive as it attracts customers or clients. But then it hits its stride and takes off. This is the growth stage and it can take a company from a small operation to a global organization. Growth is often very high in this period. Just look at the Inc. 500, *Inc.* magazine's ranking of companies with high revenue growth over a three-year period. In 2010, AtTask, which was number 500 on the list, had grown 604 percent during the previous three years. The companies on this list are fast-growth organizations, but that level of growth isn't uncommon when a business takes off. Going from $50,000 in revenue to $100,000 in revenue may not be all that difficult, but that's a 100 percent growth rate. Going from $50 million to $100 million? That's not so easy to do in one year—or even five. Unless you're Jeff Bezos, apparently, who took Amazon from $0 to $1.6 billion in a bit less than five years. In 2010 Amazon had a five-year average annual growth rate of about 37 percent for revenue and 40 percent for earnings per share. Although its rate of growth has slowed, its recent results are not too shabby.

Rapid growth is often unsustainable as a business increases in size and complexity. At almost $400 billion in revenue, Chevron would have to add $20 billion in sales to grow a mere 5 percent! Fast-growing companies eventually top out and enter maturity, attaining a growth rate that is more steady and sustainable. For instance, the five-year average sales revenue growth rate from 2007 through 2011 for the S&P 500 (large, publicly traded companies) was around 8 percent, and the earnings per share (EPS) growth rate was 7 percent. (In the last couple of years, the downturn in the economy has lowered these percentages.) Still, a mature company could move back into a high-growth period because of new products or other market expansion. Apple was one of *Fortune's* one hundred fastest-growing companies in 2011 even though it has been around for more than thirty years.

Of course, what we hope to see throughout all of these stages is growth in both the top line and the bottom line. That's a good indicator that the growth is sustainable and that the company is less likely to suddenly crash and burn. Companies that have strong cash positions, good profit margins, and asset strength have the foundation to support growth both in the short and long term.

Companies of all sizes, industries, and product-service mixes can grow both revenues and profits consistently, but sometimes they fail to do so. Shown here is a chart of Walmart's impressive revenue-growth record over nineteen years compared to that of Sears Holding, two competitors in the same industry. One creates spectacular revenue growth; the other doesn't. The difference is management's approach to vision and execution.

For its fiscal year ending January 2011, Walmart grew its revenues to $421.8 billion, more than 3 percent over prior year sales of $408 billion. Although the growth rate has slowed for Walmart during 2010 and 2011, it still grew by more than $13 billion in a struggling economy. That increase is almost equal to the current size—in terms of total revenue—of Toys "R" Us.

Revenue Growth

While fast growth can be a wonderful thing, it can often require risky investments. Lots of companies never make it past the start-up stage, and of those that make it into the growth phase, many don't make it to maturity. To grow, every company has to take some risks, and if the leaders miscalculate, those risks can result in the demise of the company. What makes all the difference is the skill of the leaders in establishing a vision for the company, creating sound strategy based on that vision, and then executing the strategy successfully. Steve Jobs retirement as CEO of Apple in August of 2011 and his subsequent passing two months later received a lot of attention because he exhibited such an amazing combination of vision, strategy, and execution.

The execution of growth strategies is where every person in the organization plays an important role. Every function can contribute to reducing costs to improve profits, to driving quality improvement, and to improving customer service, all of which contribute to either top-line or bottom-line growth.

INSIGHTS INTO GROWTH

- Companies either continue to grow or risk dying. Companies growing profitably tend to be more energized, innovate products and services, expand market share, and attract motivated top talent.

- Your CEO's most important job is to ensure sustainable, profitable growth in order to create value for owners/shareholders.

- Companies not growing can enter a "downward decline and die" cycle of higher costs, lower sales, lost market share, lower share price, cost cutting, reduction in force, demoralized employees, lost productivity, lost customers, more loss of market share, and so on. The competition will take over their markets, customers, brand positioning, and even their best people.

- The investment community looks primarily at the sales and earnings growth of a company when valuing its stock price.

- Growth is reflected primarily on a company's income statement. Both top-line growth (increasing revenue), and bottom-line growth (increasing profits) are essential over time. Top-line growth in sales does not necessarily mean bottom-line growth in profits. Over time, growth in profits is more important than growth in revenue.

- Organic growth means internal expansion—opening new stores, selling more products, and entering new demographic or geographic markets. Inorganic growth means merging with or acquiring new businesses to increase revenue.

- Growth expectations may change based on a company's stage of development. High growth may be realistic in the early years but may be less sustainable as the company matures and becomes larger and more complex.

- Risks of high growth include expenses that grow faster than sales revenue, a decline in quality, and burnout among employees. Many companies grow sales rapidly but lose money and go out of business.

Chapter 5

PEOPLE

In business, you get what you want by giving other people what they want.
—Alice MacDougall

When new employees of Nordstrom arrive for orientation, they receive a binder with the word *Welcome* on the cover and the following message, with emphasis as shown, on the first page:

> As we travel along the road of **life**, we encounter paths that lead to a great opportunity for **growth**. To recognize the doors that open to a bright **future** is the key. Once inside, we crave **support** from our colleagues. We know that the **health** of our relationships is paramount to our own **success**, and that the **joy** of sharing ideas leads to a **diversity** of options. Our reward is access to a **wealth** of knowledge that we would have otherwise overlooked. **Welcome** to Nordstrom. Our door is open.

In addition to the orientation binder, Nordstrom has an employee handbook. It is a 5½-inch by 7½-inch card with seventy-five words and only one rule: "Use good judgment in all situations."

And that is exactly what employees do. Which is why no discussion of stellar customer service can omit Nordstrom—perhaps one of the best examples of anticipating, meeting, and exceeding customer needs in its century of retail operations. Robert Spector and Patrick McCarthy, authors of *The Nordstrom Way to Customer Service Excellence* (Wiley, 2005), provide this account of how a customer, who fell in love with a pair of Donna Karan pants that were on sale, was serviced:

> The store was out of her size, and the salesperson was unable to track down a pair at the five other Nordstrom stores in the Seattle area. Aware that the same slacks were available across the street at a competitor, the salesperson secured some petty cash from her department manager, marched across the street to a competing retailer, where she bought the slacks (at full price), returned to Nordstrom and then sold them to the customer for the marked-down Nordstrom price. (p. 28)

Nordstrom's culture encourages these "heroics," and the resulting benefits of employee and customer loyalty have been profound.

In our graphic model of the 5 Key Drivers, we place people in the middle because people make the decisions, supply the financial resources, buy the products, provide the labor and services, and otherwise create and contribute to everything else about a business. They drive cash, profit, assets and growth.

Meeting, exceeding, or even better, *anticipating* the wants, needs, and expectations of your employees, customers, and other important stakeholders is essential to your financial success. People are your business, and of all your stakeholders, employees and customers are the most important. Most organizations recognize the need to satisfy both employees and customers. However, your satisfaction level in life and in business is not so much a function of the *results* you achieve, as it is a function of your *expectations* concerning those results.

Suppose your boss calls you in and gives you a $1,000 year-end bonus. Are you a happy camper? If you had been expecting a $100 bonus, you are thrilled to receive $1,000! However, if you had been counting on at least $10,000 and had already maxed out your credit cards for a vacation, new furniture, or down payment on a car, you are definitely not pleased!

Satisfaction Primarily Reflects Expectations, Not Results

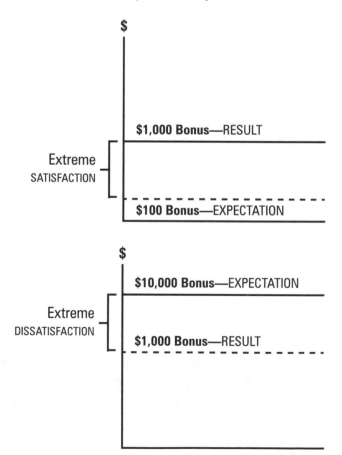

In each case, you receive exactly the same result: a $1,000 bonus. But you experience vastly different satisfaction levels based on your expectation. It is the same with employees and customers of any business.

We often can't control the circumstances influencing our employees' or customers' expectations. However, we can do much to discover and manage those expectations, because an important thing for any business is to perform consistently according to them. If you can do that, you can encourage and maximize satisfaction, and therefore loyalty, to your business. And the actual results you deliver will be spectacular! Consider the following wisdom from Maya Angelou: "People will forget what you said, people will forget what you did, but people will never forget how you made them feel."

EMPLOYEES: THE FOUNDATION OF SUCCESS

Google has what is possibly the most rigorous hiring system of any company in the history of business. Most people go through more than ten interviews before they are hired. Applicants also undergo rigorous testing. While the business world is torn about Google's practices—some saying they're eliminating the most qualified applicants, some saying they are brilliant—people line up in droves to apply. Why? Because of the way Google treats its employees.

Google expects great things. It wants brilliant people who can come up with innovative ideas that anticipate trends in the market and the future desires of Google customers. To make those goals possible, Google encourages employees, specifically its engineers, to spend 20 percent of their time dreaming up new ideas, not working on current projects. The Google "campus" is a massive complex that offers employees free gourmet meals, a twenty-four-hour fitness center, a nutritionist, an in-house doctor, a personal trainer, a swimming pool, a spa, a dry cleaner, massage therapists, and a Wi-Fi-equipped biodiesel shuttle for people who have longer commutes.

Why does Google offer these things?

Two reasons: They want to attract the very best people with the best ideas. And if they offer all of these services, employees don't have to leave the campus to access them. So, more convenience for employees and more work performed for Google.

Google isn't the only company to recognize that having great employees who contribute to a company's success has to begin with hiring the right employees. I recently heard the CEO of Zappos, Tony Hsieh, describe how his organization's hiring process is focused heavily on how well a person will fit into the company culture and support its vision of "delivering happiness." Once a person makes it through the hiring process, he or she begins training, including being on the phones for two weeks—no matter the role. But here is what I thought was most interesting. After this initial on-boarding process, Zappos actually makes an offer to the new employee of $3,000—to leave! This offer forces employees to really reflect on the question of whether this is the company they want to be a part of. In a sense, it requires them to recommit to the company. Tony explained that those employees who reject this offer and stay come back the next day with a renewed sense of commitment and ownership.

You know the old saying, "A's hire A's and B's hire C's." The best companies have a way of attracting the best people, and the best people help create even better companies.

The Number-One Reason Good Employees Leave

In his book *First, Break All The Rules*—written with coauthor Curt Coffman—Marcus Buckingham of the Gallup Organization described the results of surveys of tens of thousands of people. Those surveys revealed that the number-one reason employees leave their jobs is their relationship with their manager. While perks are great, how people feel about their managers is much more important to employee satisfaction. If they feel valued, receive regular praise, are rewarded for their efforts, are included in decision making, and feel that they are contributing to a clear vision, they are far more likely to stay. Employees who feel that leadership doesn't know where it's headed and who feel they aren't valued always have one foot out the door.

A May 2011 *USA Today* article ("Employee Loyalty Is at a Three-Year Low") stated, "Fed up, workers are seeking greener professional pastures: Slightly more than one in three hope to find a new job in the next 12 months." This attitude is surprising in a down economy. But what most leaders should be concerned about is another point the article makes: Employers are generally unaware of these high dissatisfaction levels. The best thing managers can do is take a personal interest in the career aspirations of their employees.

With the recent recession-induced focus on cost cutting, which often impacts employee pay, benefits, job security, and morale, companies need to reconsider how they will keep their good employees; if they don't, they could face an exodus.

The Value of a Good Culture

In many companies, a strong, positive, employee-focused culture helps ensure that employees get the relationships they want with management and other perks that might outweigh, say, the importance of salary. Of course, few companies are big enough or profitable enough to offer the types of perks Google offers to its employees. But every company can use its resources wisely to create a culture and offer benefits that attract top talent. A small company that can't afford to offer extensive benefits might offer a fun work environment, flexible hours, the option to bring kids to work, or a variety of other features.

In tough economic conditions, "doing more with less" is a popular catch phrase. But if you try to do too much more with much less, you risk burnout in your people. Will better equipment and tools improve their productivity without causing a stressful work environment? What about more education? It's hard to consider investments like these when you're facing financial uncertainty, but many productive and profitable companies attribute their success in part to their commitment to ongoing employee training and education—in good times and bad.

For the Ritz-Carlton (a division of Marriott International since 1997), employee education and training is key to the company's fabled success in guest satisfaction, which I'll discuss in a few pages. The company conducts continuing detailed analysis of all aspects of its operations, involving employees at every level. Ritz-Carlton has identified 970 potential problems that may arise with overnight guests. First-year managers and employees receive 250 to 300 hours or more of training on how to handle these issues. Ritz-Carlton enjoys the lowest turnover rate of any luxury hotel chain in the industry.

General Electric is another great example of a company with a strong focus on employee development, spending more than $1 billion a year developing its people, even in a "recession" economy. *Business Week* recently rated GE as the best at developing leaders, a reflection of its investment and efforts.

While culture and work environment are important factors of employee satisfaction, management can only set an example and establish goals. It's up to every employee to work to sustain a positive workplace culture.

Internal Customers

The idea of employees as "internal customers"—both of the company and of each other—has gained popularity in the past few decades. It reflects the realization that the most successful companies have the best employees and the longest tenures within their workforces. Recent studies on the cost of turnover—from $5,000 for a minimum wage position to 200 percent of annual salary for a leadership position—helped emphasize the importance of keeping valuable employees happy. And as Stephen R. Covey said, "Always treat your employees exactly as you want them to treat your best customer."

Just as many business leaders now think of employees as customers, many employees recognize that their colleagues are also their customers. Your internal customers are the people you work with or serve within your organization; you are the internal customer to others who serve and work with you. Who are *your* internal customers? Are you meeting their needs and exceeding their expectations? What are you doing to anticipate their future needs? Are you prepared to meet those needs? Have you performed surveys or analysis of how well you're doing and where you are headed in serving your internal customers? Do you hold periodic meetings to discuss process improvement, including how to enhance communication and cooperation between yourself and your internal customers?

My firm, Acumen Learning, has surveyed thousands of people and asked about their internal customers (their colleagues). The results consistently show that departments or individual employees say they provide service to their internal customers at a superior level than those internal customers say they receive. We tend to judge others by their *actions*, while we judge ourselves by our *intentions*. However, as with external customers, perception is reality—and the only reality that counts is the perception of our customers concerning the level of product or service they receive. They will make future purchase or employment decisions based on those perceptions. When is the last time you asked an internal department or a colleague you serve about their level of satisfaction with your work and what their needs are? If you aren't asking this question several times a year, you may be missing an opportunity.

It is often a primary role of human resources departments to ensure employee satisfaction and internal customer efficiency by implementing effective training programs, feedback mechanisms, and facilitating interdepartmental dialogue. But all businesspeople need to focus on how to develop and keep valuable employees and how to offer great internal service to one another. While revenue comes from customers, customers come from employees. And both are expensive to replace.

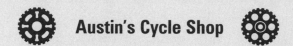

Austin's Cycle Shop

Austin had received the funding he needed to expand his operations, but now he needed to make some important decisions about how to combine operations in three locations: his current store, a new store, and an acquired store.

Austin talked regularly with his own employees about how they felt about working for him and what could be improved for greater customer and employee satisfaction. He surveyed his current customers and customers of the acquired shop and found that they would like to hear more about cycling tips, deals, great rides, and more from Austin and his employees. Austin decided to get the employees involved in creating a regular e-mail newsletter to build a more loyal customer base and give employees an opportunity to be creative and share their knowledge.

He needed to spend more time training and coaching his employees in how to create a more complete customer experience, one that was consistent across all locations. He had never created a real training program before, but as he began searching for new employees for the new stores, he knew it was time. An important point of that training would be helping his employee teams work effectively together, in addition to thinking of the employees in other stores as internal customers.

He wanted to keep key people for the long term, so he began to look at competitive wages and benefits. And he began a career path discussion with each of his employees to better plan for their future growth—so that his business could grow profitably.

CUSTOMERS: BEYOND SATISFACTION

As essential and important as internal customers are to any business, they are there to serve the "external customers"—the people who pay for your products and services, keeping your business alive. A sign on the wall of a business I frequent got it right: "Our customers are not a distraction *from* our business . . . they *are* our business."

Sam Walton, founder of Walmart, one of the largest corporations and private sector employers in the United States, established the company's strategic focus: His business is "all about the customer." Walmart's commitment to provide a better quality of life for its customers through their consistent cost savings is an essential key to the company's long-term success.

Customers are your lifeblood, your source of revenue and cash flow. Without customers, you are ultimately out of business. As Tom Peters, author of *The Pursuit of Wow!*, states, you need to wow your customers every day. Or your competitors will. And depending upon the industry in which you operate, the cost of getting a new customer is *two to ten times more* than the cost of keeping an existing customer, so you really want to keep the customers you have.

Ritz-Carlton regularly ranks among the highest luxury hotel chains in the annual hotel-guest-satisfaction survey conducted by J.D. Power and Associates. It was number one in this category in 2007, 2008, and 2010, and number two in 2009. It is the only two-time winner of the Malcolm Baldrige National Quality Award in the service category. Throughout this small luxury hotel chain, one strategic goal is 100 percent customer retention. Every employee, each of whom has been trained at the highest level, is empowered to spend up to $2,000—without checking with anyone, using only his or her best judgment—to immediately correct any problem or handle any guest complaint.

But to proactively fix problems and avoid having to pay to correct too many of them, Ritz-Carlton also performs regular and meaningful customer reviews to assess how well it is meeting its guests' needs and expectations. This is something your business can and should do. Of course, then you have to take action on the results.

Anticipation and Innovation

Most businesses try to satisfy customer needs and expectations. Other enterprises even make a conscious effort to exceed them. But truly successful companies achieve an even higher level of excellence, a more powerful form of competitive advantage. They *anticipate* the needs of customers and innovate to meet those future needs. Microsoft's "Where do you want to go today?" campaign has practical financial relevance.

While it is critical to continually survey customers and other stakeholders to determine their needs, recommendations, and desire for future products and services, that only tells you what the client is thinking right now. Customer feedback has limitations because people can't always identify what it is they'll want in the future. But strategically, you can't plan for right now; you have to plan for the future if you want to ensure your company's survival.

Effectively using the principle of *anticipation and innovation* is the ultimate competitive advantage. Dr. W. Edwards Deming, management and quality guru, said, "Innovation comes from the producer—not from the customer" and pointed out that no customer asked for a microwave oven. Henry Ford said that if he'd asked his customers what they wanted, they would've asked for a faster horse.

The innovative thinking of entrepreneurs—regardless of the size or maturity of their company—leads the consumer marketplace. Pocket-sized cell phones, GPS navigation, iPods, ebooks, and tablet computers are just a few examples of game-changing product innovations from producers over the last decade.

What happens to companies that fail to anticipate or meet customer needs? Can a big, strong, powerful, dominating company fail to anticipate in its industry, fall from competitive grace, lose leadership position and opportunities, and become relegated to "also ran" status?

General Motors, Ford, and Chrysler dominated the U.S. and international passenger-vehicle markets for decades. In 2008 GM lost its top sales position to Toyota, and in 2009 GM and Chrysler received multibillion-dollar bailouts from the federal government and filed for bankruptcy. In their 2008 fiscal years, GM lost $31 billion and Ford lost $14 billion. In 2007 the majority interest in Chrysler was sold to a private equity firm after its parent for nine years, Daimler AG, tired of its continued losses. In June of 2011, the U.S. government sold its remaining stake in Chrysler to Fiat. Why have the Big Three declined so dramatically? Because over the years they have consistently missed the customer demand for cost-effective, fuel-efficient, high-quality cars, trucks, and SUVs that exhibit appealing style and features. But the Japanese automakers anticipated American consumer desires and have captured major market share.

In September of 2010, Blockbuster filed for bankruptcy. In February of 2011, Borders filed for bankruptcy. These once-dominant organizations didn't anticipate the shift in how people would view movies and read books. History is full of many more examples of companies that failed because they failed to anticipate. As Albert Einstein said, "The significant problems we face today cannot be resolved at the same level of thinking we were at when we created them."

Of course, on the flip side you have companies like Apple. Not surprisingly, *Fortune* and *Fast Company* both listed Apple as the most innovative company in the world in 2010. Nobody can anticipate customer needs and desires better than Apple, and as *Fast Company* put it, they chose Apple for "dominating the business landscape."

Anticipating customer needs is essential for product and service innovation. The Ritz-Carlton has a deliberate program of data capture and analysis after each guest's visit, information they use to anticipate the needs of returning guests. From desired room temperature, to type and firmness of pillow and mattress, to preferred morning newspaper, fulfilling guest needs is the focus not only of the current stay, but for every future stay.

What innovative ideas can *you* contribute to your business in anticipating customer needs?

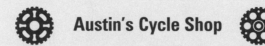

Austin's Cycle Shop

Austin needed to make sure the new store and the acquired shop were set up to maximize revenue and profit. The key, he knew, was identifying what customers in these neighborhoods were looking for.

He regularly surveyed his own customers, but the needs of his new customers would be different because the demographics of the neighborhoods were very different. In his current shop, he mostly catered to sport cyclists, so he carried high-performance bikes. Near the college campus, he'd be dealing with a younger demographic made up of people who didn't have as much cash to spend. He reviewed the sales history for the acquired shop and his assessment was confirmed. The inventory of high-performance bikes had a poor turnover rate, but the lower-cost models had strong sales numbers. He decided to keep a few high-performance models on hand but to focus his inventory on a range of affordable bicycles. He would also begin selling scooters, because they were very popular with college students.

In the new shop, he would be in the middle of a highly residential neighborhood. He spent some time in the new neighborhood, watching families who were out and about. Cycling among families seemed common, and so he knew he would need to sell kids' bikes. It was a fairly affluent neighborhood, and there was a broad range of higher-end kids' bikes that were highly adjustable and designed to last for a long time. He had also seen some innovative baby carriers from his suppliers that he thought would be good sellers. And it seemed like touring bikes would be a good idea for the adult inventory, with some high-performance bikes and parts on hand for the local fanatics.

One thing that surprised him was the number of scooters he saw in the neighborhood. He hadn't anticipated that. He decided that he would also offer scooters at the new store, which would give him greater leverage in negotiating with suppliers.

What Are Your Customers Really Buying?

What do your customers really want or need? Perhaps they don't truly know. To answer the question, you can begin by considering what they are *actually* buying. If you think about it deeply enough, you may find that your customers are buying something deeper than you thought, something more than just a simple product or service. Knowing what product or service your customer is really buying becomes all-important in managing expectations and in anticipating needs.

When families eat out, are parents buying hamburgers, or are they buying a fun outing with the kids? Customers buy automobiles not just for transportation but also for status and prestige. They buy clothing to make personal statements. Why do customers buy your products and services? What do they *really* want or need? They probably are paying for convenience, reliability, value, prestige, time savings, and other intangible benefits that may or may not be related to a product's actual use or application.

McDonald's started off by selling exactly the same hamburger you could get in almost any restaurant. Today they sell a fun family experience, complete with toys and playground—with hamburgers and other menu items on the side. Starbucks started off by providing the opportunity to participate in a social experience patterned after the coffee houses of Italy. At my business, Acumen Learning, one client, a large wireless phone company, indicated that cell phones are one of the top five status symbols for teens—in other words, their parents are paying for much more than the functionality of the phone. SUVs and minivans aren't sold so much for transportation as to facilitate a lifestyle. (And why did it take car manufacturers so many years to figure out that sliding doors on both sides of a minivan might be a good idea?)

Anyone in business-to-business sales knows that it's an absolute necessity to understand what your customer is really buying from you. Why? In the B2B world, you can benefit greatly from knowing how your customer's business creates profits. If you understand the 5 Key Drivers as applied to your customer, and then show how your product or service can impact a combination of your customer's cash, profit, assets, growth, and people, you will enjoy a significant sales advantage because you understand what it is your customer is really buying—improved business performance.

A top executive at one of the largest computer manufacturers recently said to me, "My salespeople can speak all day long about the features of our products. I need them to tell their customers how it will help them improve their profits." Our course helped this company's salespeople connect the product features with the bottom-line results those features could provide. At the end of the day, this is what the customer wants to know.

Customers often don't recognize their own needs or how to meet them; they don't recognize the possibilities. Keeping current customers and attracting new ones means anticipating needs that they might never articulate.

No company is immune to market failure and loss of industry leadership. It is essential to always study and anticipate customer needs, and to invest in the technology and marketing capability to remain competitive. Just as important, cultivating teamwork inside the organization ensures that internal customers will be better able to serve the external ones. Understanding how your company benefits from its relationship with its most crucial asset—people—can help you impact stakeholder satisfaction and the bottom line, whether you're the CEO or new hire fresh out of college.

💡 INSIGHTS INTO PEOPLE

- People are the most important resource for any company. Employees and customers are two important stakeholders to your business.

- Successful companies usually have a history of strong employee satisfaction and longer employee tenure, so companies work hard to keep employees satisfied and to attract top talent.

- Internal customers are those employees or departments to whom we provide work product, information, or output. Most employees are both internal suppliers and internal customers to each other.

- Satisfaction and loyalty are more a result of expectations met than actual results achieved. Managing customer expectations is critical in creating loyalty. Delivering on the expectations is essential.

- Your customers are the lifeblood of your business. You should focus on your customers more than on your competitors.

- Anticipating and innovating to meet unstated present and future customer needs is a key to long-term competitive success.

- Most innovative, breakthrough products are a result not of customer requests but of innovative anticipation of unexpressed customer needs and opportunities in the marketplace.

- Customers buy more than just products. They purchase trustworthiness, convenience, prestige, or a memorable experience. Determine what *your* customers are buying.

Chapter 6

THE BIG PICTURE: LINKING THE 5 DRIVERS

The whole is more than the sum of its parts.
—Aristotle

For six decades, Toyota generated profits year after year. Then, in 2009, its record crumbled under the pressure of the global recession and it booked its first annual net loss—of $7.7 billion. For some companies, this loss might have signaled their demise. But Toyota has excelled in ways that have helped it weather what was just the beginning of a violent storm. What are the keys to the company's success? Asset strength, a clear vision of what consumers want now and in the future, consistent revenue growth, and maximum efficiency in asset utilization to generate profits and cash. The company understood each of the 5 Key Drivers—cash, profit, assets, growth, and people.

The recession was just the first of many hits to come. A massive recall in 2009 and 2010 to solve an accelerator problem (which some claim was the result of an overdeveloped focus on controlling costs). A fine from the U.S. government of almost $16 million for not alerting officials to the problem early enough. And then, the horrific earthquake that hit Japan in March 2011, causing heartbreak and devastation for Toyota's home country. And from a business perspective, an ongoing loss of production as suppliers are unable to fill orders.

Despite the hits that kept coming, Toyota focused on what it knew best: making cars people wanted as efficiently as possible. It declared a state of profit emergency in 2009 and took drastic measures to book a profit in 2010. The plan?

- Deliver more eco-friendly vehicles (more hybrid models) and piggyback on government promotion (tax breaks, for instance)
- Introduce special editions to meet the specific needs of consumers in certain regions
- Cut variable costs by about $3.5 billion by reducing costs at manufacturing plants, among other strategies
- Cut fixed costs by about $4.75 billion by reducing capital expenditures (it closed and sold a major plant, for instance)
- Reduce R&D expenses by streamlining product development
- Reduce G&A costs, such as travel expenses
- Improve labor efficiency by implementing job sharing and other measures

Did it work?

Absolutely. Despite the continued global economic crisis, the company earned $2.2 billion in 2010 and over $5 billion in 2011 as a result of its efforts. If Toyota had not been stronger financially, if its asset position had been weaker, if its operations had been less efficient, if its customers had had a poor opinion of the company, if it hadn't been growing steadily for decades, it would never have been able to achieve this one-year turnaround in profit.

A company that excels in any one driver must also excel in others—and frequently, in all of them. The 5 Key Drivers, as we've seen in the previous five chapters, are completely interdependent; over the long-term, it is impossible to be excellent in one and severely deficient in the others. Any change in one driver affects the others.

DIVISION OF LABOR, UNITY OF PURPOSE

So often in our attempts to get on the same page, we overlook the fact that organizations—like books—have many different pages. It's how all of the pages combine to create the entire book, or the entire organization, that is most important. In your company (and most others), the various functions and departments (the pages) have different areas of focus, specific divisions of labor. But when they work together, they should all have unity of purpose.

The following chart shows some of the key functions that exist in many organizations and the drivers they usually focus on.

Function	Primary Focus
Sales	People (customers), profit (revenue), growth
Human resources	People (employees), growth (by attracting the best employees)
Finance	Cash, profit, assets, growth
Marketing	Growth (through increased sales)
Facilities management	Assets, growth
Information technology	Assets, growth
Customer service	People (customers), growth
Senior leadership	Growth, profit, people, cash, assets
CEO	Growth, profit, people, cash, assets

It's entirely appropriate for different functions to focus on the 5 Key Drivers in different ways at different times. But with this focus, they need to make sure they are not sub-optimizing the whole. They must continually see the big picture and understand how their actions are affecting all of the drivers. You can see from the chart above that most senior leaders and CEOs of public companies focus primarily on growth and profit, as these tend to drive stock prices higher. You will often hear CEOs state that the goal of the company is something like "To build a profitable, growing, and enduring company."

It seems simple when presented, but not so obvious in daily practice. When you talk with people in other departments, look at the issue or topic at hand from their perspective and from their functional responsibility. One of the most important applications of business acumen is communicating with colleagues from other departments on the basis of what's important to them. When a human resources officer speaks with a finance manager about a key initiative, talking about employee satisfaction might result in impatient yawns. However, discussing cost of capital, return on investment, and the expense reductions realized from the initiative will get the finance manager's attention. If you connect with what's important to people in other departments, they'll pay more attention to your ideas.

SHIFTING FOCUS: THE URGENCY CONTINUUM

CEOs, senior leaders and managers, and the company as a whole naturally shift focus among the five drivers over time along an *urgency continuum*. Depending on the stage of an organization's development, and based upon complex internal and external factors throughout a company's history, senior management gives priority to different drivers at different times. Remember Toyota's laser focus on profit in 2010. And when a company makes a huge purchase—as Google did when it announced plans to purchase Motorola Mobility in 2011—it is in a way shifting its focus away from cash and toward assets and growth. Another example occurred in 2008, when banks shifted their focus away from profits and growth and toward cash in an effort to strengthen their financial position during the Great Recession.

Now, just because a company shifts its focus from one driver to another doesn't mean that the company loses focus on the other drivers. For example, a company in crisis that needs to focus on cash shouldn't ignore its customers or forget about long-term growth. In fact, a renewed customer focus might be necessary to generate the critical cash required for an investment in assets necessary to fuel long-term growth.

CEO Urgency Continuum

URGENT	NEAR TERM	LONG TERM
CASH	PROFIT ASSETS	GROWTH PEOPLE

Urgent: Cash. In the start-up stage of a company's history, the need for cash is typically the urgent focus of management, possibly superseding all other priorities. But the start-up years aren't the only time a company might be focused on cash. In 1993 when Lou Gerstner took over as CEO of deeply troubled IBM, he said the company's mission was to "survive." In his book *Who Says Elephants Can't Dance* (HarperCollins, 2002), he said that few people understood how perilously close IBM came to running out of cash.

During an economic crisis, like the one that began in December 2007, many companies focus much more on cash so that they can feel secure in their ability to ride out the worst to come, particularly when credit and capital are hard to come by. But when a company focuses on cash, what does that mean? Often it means conserving cash by cutting costs and investments to improve profitability, which will likely slow future growth.

Near Term: Profit and Assets. In the normal development of a business, leaders want to reach a point where cash flow from operations meets normal cash requirements. Once this point is reached, companies will often zero in on profit-generating initiatives and investments in assets to build asset strength. A management team can then focus more time and energy on creating greater profit margins and using its assets more efficiently to obtain a greater return on investment.

Long Term: Growth and People. Ultimately, a CEO wants to focus the company on attracting the best employees and customers, creating long-term, sustainable, profitable growth. When Apple purchased the music streaming business LaLa in 2009, Apple's management was upfront about the fact that one of its primary reasons for purchasing the company was LaLa's engineers. Mature companies that have cash, consistent profits, and asset strength have a solid foundation that allows them to concentrate on growth and people strategies that continue to move the company forward in the long term.

Shifting With the Company

Any time you impact any of the 5 Key Drivers, you are impacting the overall success of your company. The question is, are you having the *maximum* impact and the *right* impact? For instance, if senior leadership says that profitability is all-important this quarter and asks employees to identify ways to reduce costs, you should certainly follow that lead. However, you have to apply your business acumen to make smart, productive decisions. Cutting costs too much could adversely affect product and service quality, reducing customer satisfaction and leading to lower sales and profits. And if you were responsible for increasing revenue to improve profitability, raising prices too high or using cash to launch product lines without sufficient research and analysis into customer tastes could result in lower sales and profits.

Every businessperson should ask the following questions to make sure that his or her daily decisions and activities are contributing in the best and most efficient way possible:

- "Which driver is the most important for our company (and why)?"

- "How can I impact this driver? What resources do I need?"

- "What effect on each of the other drivers will this action have?"

- "How can the impact be measured?"

If you think about these questions regularly, you'll stand out among your peers and prove your value to the organization.

THE 5 DRIVERS IN A PUBLIC COMPANY

Unlike the head of a private company, the CEO of a publicly traded corporation faces unique pressures that influence the entire organization. First, all important actions that he or she takes are publicly visible through full-disclosure reporting to the SEC and to shareholders. Second, the CEO's most important job becomes increasing shareholder value, which means making the stock price increase over time. Investors often have a short-term focus and want to see growth *every quarter*. Frequently, decisions that might increase short-term stock price are not necessarily in the company's long-term best interests.

The level of oversight, reporting requirements, government compliance, legal and accounting obligations, and consequences for failure to comply are far more complex and rigid for a public company than for one that is privately owned. The annual expense of meeting these requirements—legal, accounting, and otherwise—is very heavy.

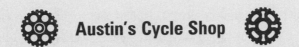

It had been two years since Austin acquired a competitor and opened a new store. He had developed growing brand recognition for his excellent products and services. He focused more and more on expanding his customer base and on the continued growth of his business.

The various stores excelled in different ways, but he wanted all of his employees to be focused on his vision for the company: a new type of bicycle shop, focused on the highest levels of service, that could grow locally, regionally, and even nationally. He began having regular all-staff meetings with his employees to share how the company was doing overall and what types of challenges each store was facing. The meetings were also intended to get employees involved in discovering solutions to those challenges and in finding opportunities to grow the business.

After the first few meetings, the employees seemed to catch on to Austin's vision and offered up interesting ideas for increasing growth and profitability, including a dynamic cross-store inventory-management system that would help any store meet any customer's needs quickly.

This process helped Austin discover his new overall vision for the company: to create a national brand and one day take the company public. How? Take the company online, selling bikes and parts to a broad range of customers—customers whose needs he better understood through the development of his various shops. But he knew he would need to go even further to offer unique products and services to bicycle enthusiasts.

Austin sought out another investor who could offer the capital he needed to hire an online retail-consulting firm. The consultants helped him hire the right Web developers, assess marketing approaches and possible partnerships, and anticipate capital and asset needs. He developed relationships with custom bicycle manufacturers as well as local retailers in key geographic areas, which helped him offer a level of service unlike anything the other online retailers could match. He was even able to develop his own line of branded bicycles by working with the major manufacturers.

It took a couple of years to really achieve success through his online venture. Once he had, he decided to take his privately held company public. He needed increased access to both equity and debt capital from public markets to grow his earnings.

Austin would have a lot of expenses as his company went through an Initial Public Offering (IPO). There would be added overhead costs, plus the time he would have to devote to complying with SEC regulations and reporting requirements. He would have to focus on delivering consistently increasing quarterly earnings so that investors would see his company as a growth stock and push the price higher.

However, he felt that the benefits outweighed the costs. As he looked at the competitive landscape, he felt that by becoming a public company he would have a significant advantage over locally owned cycle shops and small online retailers—he could grow more rapidly and profitably. He wanted to become the Amazon of bikes—and steal bike business away from Amazon!

He began working on the IPO with a securities broker-dealer and attorneys.

From personal lessons learned, Austin knew that despite becoming a public company he would have to continue his focus on the 5 Key Drivers— the foundation of his future success. The big picture of Austin's Cycle Shop was expanding, but the fundamentals would never change.

THE EVEN BIGGER PICTURE: THE EXTERNAL ENVIRONMENT

While maximizing the 5 Key Drivers is the central tenet of business acumen, you must consider other factors, external to your business, when trying to make smart, effective decisions. The dynamics of such influences as the national economy, your competitors, industry issues, and the political and social environment are critical to your company's success. Within this broader framework, leaders make real-world decisions and exercise their best business judgment. Your fundamental grasp of the external environment is essential to connecting the dots and applying your own acumen.

The environment in which your business operates is characterized by *dynamic change*. In fact, external factors are the primary cause of cyclical changes in the growth or profitability of many organizations, because the growth or contraction of the overall economy tends to be cyclical and ever changing. Your company must continually adjust, innovate, and even reinvent itself to keep pace with the uncertain complexities of the economic, political, social, and business environment.

Most of what goes on in the external environment is beyond the direct control or even influence of your company or any company—even giants like Apple, GE, Microsoft, and Walmart. But that doesn't mean that business leaders are powerless. As Stephen R. Covey says, "You cannot always control what happens to you, but you can control your response to it." Even without being able to control these factors, a business can anticipate, prepare, and choose its strategic response to them.

Nokia, for instance, completely missed a market it could have dominated. "Everyone underestimated how incredibly successful the iPhone would be," said Dan Hesse, who was a director on Nokia's board when the device was first launched. "We took the iPhone seriously, but Nokia management underestimated it, certainly" (Greg Bensinger, "Sprint CEO on Jobs," *Wall Street Journal*, August 25, 2011). Once the worldwide leader in handset sales, Nokia has fallen to number three. While Nokia focused on competing with RIM's BlackBerry device, Steve Jobs built the iconic iPhone and articulated what he called a post-PC era of iPads, app stores, and cloud-based services. Nokia and RIM executives neither grasped the changing needs of customers nor embraced the evolving technology to meet them, and now these category creators are finding it difficult to even be competitive in the category they helped to create.

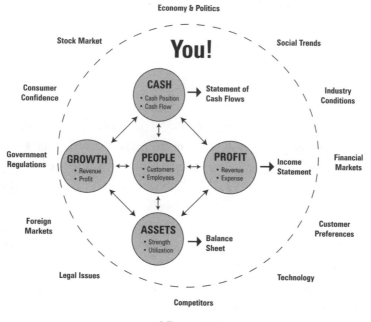

... and External Factors

As you continue to study the environment in which your business operates, keep asking yourself, "What changes are about to take place, and how will they likely impact the 5 Key Drivers of my business? How can we successfully be prepared for the threats and take advantage of the opportunities?" Commit to an ongoing study of what's happening in the economy, in your industry, and in the markets in which you operate. Your business acumen *must* include a working knowledge of the business world outside your company and how it might influence your future.

To get you started down that path, I'll lay the foundation for two external influencers that can affect the direction of your company.

Financial Markets

Financial markets reflect the combined impact of all the other external factors. By "financial markets" we mean the availability and cost of capital from all sources, national and international. This includes loans from banks and other institutions, borrowing money by selling debt instruments (like bonds), or raising equity capital in the stock market. Financial or money markets reflect national and international, rather than local, conditions.

In the United States, the Federal Reserve sets key interest rates and influences the supply of money nationwide. Whether a small entrepreneur in her local community can get a start-up loan or whether larger companies can raise capital to expand, and at what price and terms, is greatly influenced by federal policy. The availability and price of money affects the ability of *all* companies to grow, to innovate products, and to take needed risks; it changes access to the capital the company needs to make critical investments in assets.

Companies are just like homeowners in this way: the ability to get a mortgage loan at a local bank is impacted by federal monetary policy.

The Stock Market

For public companies, the stock market plays an important role in directing the focus of the CEO and other leaders. They want the stock price to always be increasing, and when it's not, you'll see a lot of worried frowns.

Why should they—and you—be concerned about your company's stock price? First, because your stock price is a reflection of the market's confidence in your company's future performance. People primarily buy stock because they believe they will make money as your stock price increases over time or through dividends. But a company also benefits in other ways when its stock price is higher:

- Acquisitions—When stock price is higher, the company can use fewer shares to buy another company.

- More cash from secondary offerings—When a public company sells more shares to investors in a secondary offering, it can sell a smaller percentage of the company to raise the same or greater cash if the stock price is higher.

- Better credit ratings—One of the determinants of a public company's credit ratings relates to its stock price. With higher credit ratings, it can raise debt or equity capital at lower rates and with better terms.

- Desirable stock options—An increasing stock price indicates a successful company. It can provide more desirable stock options to retain and attract smart, talented employees.

- Buy-out defense—A higher stock price is a defense against a takeover. As the stock price goes up, so does the company's value, and therefore its sales price.

In addition to being focused on growth in sales and profits, companies can influence their stock price through stock buybacks. Many companies use their excess cash to buy back their own stock, thus reducing the number of shares outstanding and increasing the earnings per share. Generally this tactic will increase the stock's market price. One justification is that buying one's own stock shows that the company management believes in itself—investing in its own stock gives the highest, safest return. This approach is intended to raise confidence for investors and encourage them to also buy the stock—increasing demand, and hopefully, the price.

Regardless of whether your company is public or private, the 5 Key Drivers and the major influences of your business environment should be the foundation of the decisions you make to keep your company on the path to profitable, sustainable growth.

INSIGHTS INTO THE BIG PICTURE

- The big picture is the overall perspective of how your company makes money through the 5 Key Drivers. It includes the context of the outside environment.

- All 5 Drivers are interdependent. Any impact on one affects the others.

- Companies known for excellence in one driver usually excel in others as well.

- Different organizational departments or functions tend to prioritize different drivers. To have influence within your company, learn to "speak the language" of people who have functional responsibilities different from your own.

- Anything you can do to impact any of the 5 Drivers influences the big picture. Among the key questions to ask is "How can I impact this driver and measure the results?"

- In addition to the impact of the 5 Key Drivers, business performance is affected by dynamic, complex forces in the external environment, including financial markets and the stock market.

PART II

Simplifying Financial Statements
Through the 5 Drivers

Chapter 7

DECIPHERING FINANCIAL STATEMENTS AND THE ANNUAL REPORT

"Rule number 1: Never lose money.
Rule number 2: Never forget rule number 1."
—Warren Buffett

A corporate health report. A moving picture of growth. Statistics that help predict the outcome of the next move, the next growth strategy. All of these analogies—medical, movies, sports—have been used by authors and others (including me) to help people get a better sense of what financial statements really mean and why they are important in the business world. And just like in medicine or movie editing or baseball, for the uninitiated, financial statements can seem overwhelming.

But they don't have to be. The key is to understand that, unless you're a CFO or a financial analyst or a commercial loan manager, you don't have to understand everything in these statements to discover important clues about the health and sustainability of a company. Throughout this and the next three chapters I'll explain what financial statements can reveal and show you the most important numbers, metrics, and measures to look for and what they mean. In this chapter, I'll also explain the basics of an annual report, which is where you will find these financial statements, at least for public companies.

AKA

The income statement, balance sheet, and statement of cash flows are often referred to collectively as *the financials*.

THE THREE MOST IMPORTANT STATEMENTS AND THE 5 KEY DRIVERS

The three financial statements (frequently called "the financials") that every public company prepares and shares are the income statement, the balance sheet, and the statement of cash flows, all of the statements I've referred to in earlier chapters. You will often hear the word *consolidated* used with these statements, which simply means that figures from all subsidiaries and business units are included in the financial statements. Public companies must file quarterly reports (Form 10-Q) and annual reports (Form 10-K) with the Securities and Exchange Commission (SEC), which are made available to the public. Privately held companies prepare these statements for tax purposes and because they help leaders and owners understand how the company is performing.

The income statement (also called the profit and loss statement or P&L) reports revenues, expenses, and "bottom line" net income, or profitability. And for public companies, it includes earnings per share of stock.

The balance sheet shows company assets, liabilities, and shareholder equity, and therefore reveals the financial strength of the company. When analyzed with the income statement, it also reveals how efficiently assets are being utilized.

The statement of cash flows reports where a company gets its cash and how it uses it in three activities: *operations* or core business activities; *investing*, by buying and selling assets; and *financing*, through receiving and paying loans, selling and repurchasing stock, or paying dividends.

These three statements connect like puzzle pieces. The income statement begins with revenues and ends with net income. Net income is the first line on the statement of cash flows, which then shows cash flowing into and out of the company to end with a calculation of the current amount of cash and cash equivalents on hand (cash position). The balance sheet then begins with cash and cash equivalents and outlines other assets and liabilities to get to a calculation of shareholder's equity. The three statements start with a reflection of the activities the firm engages in with customers (revenues) and then create a bridge to how those activities drive greater value for the shareholders (shareholder's equity).

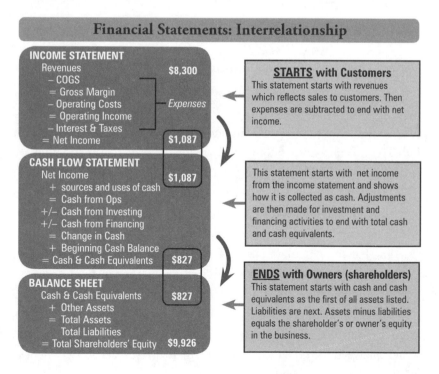

Financial Statements: Interrelationship

INCOME STATEMENT
Revenues	$8,300
– COGS	
= Gross Margin	
– Operating Costs	*Expenses*
= Operating Income	
– Interest & Taxes	
= Net Income	$1,087

STARTS with Customers
This statement starts with revenues which reflects sales to customers. Then expenses are subtracted to end with net income.

CASH FLOW STATEMENT
Net Income	$1,087
+ sources and uses of cash	
= Cash from Ops	
+/– Cash from Investing	
+/– Cash from Financing	
= Change in Cash	
+ Beginning Cash Balance	
= Cash & Cash Equivalents	$827

This statement starts with net income from the income statement and shows how it is collected as cash. Adjustments are then made for investment and financing activities to end with total cash and cash equivalents.

BALANCE SHEET
Cash & Cash Equivalents	$827
+ Other Assets	
= Total Assets	
Total Liabilities	
= Total Shareholders' Equity	$9,926

ENDS with Owners (shareholders)
This statement starts with cash and cash equivalents as the first of all assets listed. Liabilities are next. Assets minus liabilities equals the shareholder's or owner's equity in the business.

The numbers and the figure will help you see how the financial statements of Austin's Cycle Shop, presented in chapters 8, 9, and 10, tie together.

The 5 Key Drivers are not just a theoretical model of what is important to any business. As I explained in the introduction, they are based on the reports that all business leaders use to track financial performance. These financial statements are critical because they track the elements of a company that can lead to its success or its failure: cash, profit, assets, and growth over time:

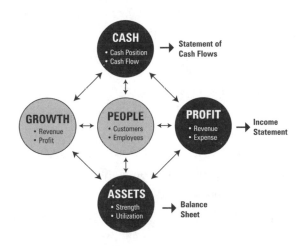

Cash: Statement of cash flows

Profit: Income statement

Assets: Balance Sheet

Growth: Companies seek to grow the results measured on all three financial statements

And of course, People: The activity that these financial statements reflect is how well *employees* are providing value to *customers*.

THE BASICS OF FINANCIAL STATEMENTS

You don't have to be a certified electrician with a deep understanding of the wiring diagram in your home to turn on a light switch. You just need to know which one or two switches control the lights you want to turn on and off, and where they are located. Similarly, you don't need to understand most of the line items on the financial statements to understand the statements' basic message. You just need to know which primary switches turn on the right financial lights—revealing the truth of a company's financial health. I'll explore those switches for each financial statement in the following chapters. I'll begin with a Big Picture Breakdown for those people who are only interested in the highlights and then dive deeper, working through line by line, for those who think they need a more in-depth understanding.

Before diving in, though, there are a few basic rules and hurdles that you should be familiar with. They will help you make sense of most financial statements.

First, recall from the discussion of accrual-basis accounting in chapter 2 that most large organizations follow that approach, which influences when revenue, expenses, and profit are "booked" or recorded in accounting systems and when they appear on financial statements.

Second, in the United States, all audited financial statements are prepared according to rules established by the accounting profession and governmental agencies. These generally accepted accounting principles (GAAP) are developed by the Financial Accounting Standards Board (FASB), a private nonprofit association of the accounting profession. The SEC requires that the financial statements of all public companies be prepared according to GAAP. These rules are also used by the IRS to calculate a company's income taxes. Companies outside of the United States often follow the International Financial Reporting Standards (IFRS).

Third, the amounts on the financial statements of larger companies are often truncated. At the top of the statements, you will see the notation "In thousands," "000s dropped," "In millions," or "000,000s dropped," which means that when you read the numbers, you must add those missing zeros to get the actual number: for example, $470 is actually $470,000 if the statement is presented in thousands and $470 million if the statement is presented in millions. For smaller companies, the exact figures are usually shown, but be careful to check for this notation so you read the financial statement figures correctly.

Fourth, even though the fundamental organization of financial statements is consistent, companies may label items differently, which can make reading them a challenge (revenue might be called net sales, for instance). The financial statements of a company in one industry might look different from those of a company in another industry. For instance, the financials of banks and financial institutions look different from those of retailers. After reviewing a few financials, however, you'll be able to understand most of the major entries. In the following chapters, I'll explain the most common line items and the different terms you might see used to communicate the same thing. Getting acquainted with your own company's terminology is important. It will be relatively constant over time.

Last, keep in mind that numbers are only meaningful within a certain context, within a larger story. So when looking at key measures on a financial statement, it may be useful to review four basic characteristics. I'll explore these for some of the key line items on each statement:

- Amount: The amount of the item, which you may want to be positive or negative, as high as possible (like revenue) or as low as possible (like cost of goods sold).

- Trend: The trend over the last two or more years. Is the item going up or down, and by what percentage? Why? Is the rate of change accelerating or slowing? Is this the right direction?

- Ratio: The ratio of the item to other relevant items. You should also look at the trend of the ratio. I'll explain what ratios to review for some of the key line items.

- Industry and competitor analysis: How do these numbers compare to the industry and key competitors? Ask why your company is doing better or worse.

To help you find your way through the most important measures, we've developed a "Navigating the Financials" graphic, shown here, which we use in our workshops. You can go to our website at www.seeingthebigpicture.com and access a PDF version of this document. There are instructions for how to use it online. In our workshops, we have found it extremely useful in helping participants better understand the relationships among the 5 Key Drivers and key company metrics found on their own financial statements.

Navigating the Financials

	KEY METRIC	Income	Balance	Cash Flow	FORMULA	RESULTS
CASH	01) Cash & Cash Equivalents Line item: Cash & Cash Equivalents		•		None	$
	02) Cash from Operations Line item: Cash from Operations			•	None	$
PROFIT	03) Total Revenue Line item: Total Revenue	•			None	$
	04) Net Income Line item: Net Income	•			None	$
	05) Net Profit Margin Line item: Net Income Line item: Total Revenue	• •			Equation $\left(\dfrac{\text{Net Income}}{\text{Total Revenue}} \right) \times 100$	%
ASSETS	06) Equity Ratio Line item: Total Shareholder Equity Line item: Total Assets		• •		Equation $\left(\dfrac{\text{Total Shareholder Equity}}{\text{Total Assets}} \right) \times 100$	%
	07) Return on Assets (ROA) Line item: Net Income Line item: Total Assets	•	•		Equation $\left(\dfrac{\text{Net Income}}{\text{Total Assets}} \right) \times 100$	%
GROWTH	08) Revenue Growth Line item: Total Revenue	•			Equation $\left(\dfrac{\text{Period* Revenue}}{\text{Prior Period* Revenue}} - 1 \right) \times 100$	%
	09) Net Income Growth Line item: Net Income	•			Equation $\left(\dfrac{\text{Period* Net Income}}{\text{Prior Period* Net Income}} - 1 \right) \times 100$	%
	10) Earnings Per Share (EPS) Growth Line item: EPS	•			Equation $\left(\dfrac{\text{Period* EPS}}{\text{Prior Period* EPS}} - 1 \right) \times 100$	%

PEOPLE: Employee business decisions and customer preferences directly impact every aspect of financial performance.

Now that you know some basics about financial reports, where can you find them? For privately held companies, the CEO might send some or all of the statements out to employees or may have a meeting with all staff to go over the key financial metrics. If you work for a small company and haven't seen the financials, you might ask your manager if it's possible to do so, or at least get a report of key metrics. If you work for a publicly held company, the financials, along with other information, are readily available in the annual report.

READING AN ANNUAL REPORT

I've already described the annual report—the Form 10-K—that public companies are required to file with the government and make available to shareholders. It consists of fifteen "items" that a company must address. The great detail and disclosure in these reports are intended to help shareholders understand the business they are investing in. Although I find much of the 10-K's content not particularly important, the following three items are very valuable in analyzing a company, particularly because this is where the financial statements live.

Item 1: Business: This section of the 10-K provides a basic overview or description of the company. It might include information about product or service lines, how it conducts business, customer information, etc. If you are a salesperson preparing to call on a client, a supply chain manager evaluating a new supplier, or a prospective employee preparing for an interview with the company, this item might be helpful.

Item 7: Management Discussion and Analysis (MD&A): Sometimes preceded by an "Overview" or called "Management's Report," this section contains a discussion of the company's performance over the last year. It also previews opportunities and potential problems with future performance. It can be lengthy and technical. But I encourage you to read it, as it discusses important happenings in the business.

Item 8: Financial Statements: Here's where you will find the three key financial statements (those that I'll explain in detail in chapters 8 through 10). The financials are accompanied by an auditor's report, a letter signed by independent accountants affirming their performance in auditing the financial statements prepared by the company management team. Usually this is a boilerplate letter, but you should scan the last couple of paragraphs for any exceptions to a "clean" report.

Also included in Item 8 are the Notes to Financial Statements, a collection of supplemental information pertaining to the financial statements. Reading the notes front-to-back is an instant cure for insomnia. However, if you have a question about line items in the financials, you will often find the answers referenced in the notes. There is important information contained in these pages.

In addition to the Form 10-K that's filed with the SEC, most public companies will produce a much more reader-friendly version of their annual report for shareholders, prospective investors, the business and financial media, and the public. Even some private companies, who are not required to file a Form 10-K, will publish an annual report to communicate to their stakeholders their assessment of the year. You'll find that, as in the financial statements, the 5 Key Drivers stand out prominently in these annual reports, possibly with one emphasized over the others at times. While no two annual reports are alike (there are no standards or rules as there are for the 10-K) you'll want to look for and read the following:

Financial Highlights. Analysts and investors often start their review of an annual report with the financial highlights; sometimes you'll find these highlights on the inside of the front cover and perhaps spilling across two or three pages. These highlights are extracted from the complete financial statements, and you'll typically see at least two years of data summarized, perhaps three or more. Key financial highlights might pertain to the 5 Key Drivers, market share, products, or other data.

CEO's Letter to Shareholders. Generally, you'll find a letter to the shareholders signed by the CEO. This letter is very important. Read it carefully. It indicates the issues and initiatives most important to the senior leadership of the company. Usually the "spin" of this letter is positive—even reporting on a bad year, the CEO might comment about how bright the future looks, or how the company is "on its way back up."

However, this letter is a good place to find out what went on during the previous year, what the outlook for the future is, and what strategies are important to the chief executive. The drivers most frequently addressed by almost every CEO in these letters are growth and profitability. Frequently CEOs reference their people by discussing the company's customers and employees. If there are specific initiatives for improving profitability, you'll find references to margins or cost containment or expense reduction. If you'll read this letter and keep a simple tally of how often cash, profit, assets, growth, and people are referenced, you'll get an idea of which drivers the CEO is focused on.

Marketing: Many annual reports are prepared with colorful photos and graphics and glowing prose explaining how wonderful the company is. They read more like a marketing brochure than a financial report—because they actually are. Like the letter from the CEO, the marketing portion of the annual report will typically have a positive spin, but reviewing this information will give you insights into the company's products, customers, and culture.

Compliance: Form 10-K. The last section of the annual report is part or all of the company's financial statements or its actual Form 10-K. It might be printed on thinner paper with black ink and no graphics, and is written in language that is obviously not intended as easy reading. If you're dealing with a public company and don't see the entire Form 10-K in your copy of the annual report, go to the company's website and look for an "Investor Relations" section, or do a search on the SEC's website (www.sec.gov/edgar).

While reading every line of a company's financials, annual report, or 10-K is almost never necessary, a review of key items is a surefire path to understanding a company's current situation, its goals, and its chances for long-term success. In the next three chapters, I'll simplify the financial statements so that you can get in and get out with what you need.

INSIGHTS INTO FINANCIAL STATEMENTS AND ANNUAL REPORTS

- The income statement, the balance sheet, and the statement of cash flows are the financial statements that reflect performance around the 5 Key Drivers. Although the financial statements of different companies are organized similarly, they may use different terms.

- When analyzing numbers on the financial statements, you should review four basic characteristics:

  1. Amount

  2. Trend

  3. Ratio (the amount compared to other numbers)

  4. Comparison to competitors and/or industry

- Public companies are required by the SEC to file Form 10-K, an annual report that contains the three key financial statements. While there are a standard fifteen items in Form 10-K, three are noteworthy:

  - Item 1: Business

  - Item 7: Management's Discussion and Analysis (MD&A)

  - Item 8: Financial Statements and Supplementary Data

- Companies may choose to release an additional annual report that's easier to read than a Form 10-K. The purpose of this annual report is to communicate company strategy, market and brand the company, and share financial highlights.

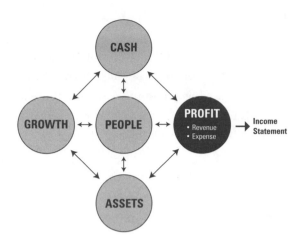

Chapter 8

INCOME STATEMENT: TRACKING PROFIT

Remind people that profit is the difference between revenue and expense.
This makes you look smart.
—Scott Adams

Imagine it's November 2008. You're a salesperson for a restaurant supply company, and Starbucks is one of your prospects. In preparation for your big pitch, you check out Starbucks' latest press releases and like what Starbucks' CEO has to say about the company's fiscal year 2008 results: "We began the new fiscal year with a healthier store portfolio that will allow for operating margin expansion. Despite a global economic environment that shows no immediate signs of improvement, the steps we took in FY08 position us to deliver EPS [earnings per share] growth in FY09 . . . We appear to be more resilient than many other premium brands. And while we cannot call isolated signs of improving sales a trend, we are encouraged by our ability to drive increased traffic at a relatively low cost . . . I am optimistic we are well positioned to weather this challenging economic environment."

It sounds like the company is on track to grow and be profitable despite the recession. This is great news for you, but later in the day a colleague sends you a link to a *Fortune* blog column that tells a different story: "Starbucks' Schultz needs to get real . . . needs less optimism and a stronger dose of reality in his brew" (Patricia Sellers, November 11, 2008).

Youch! Which is it? How are you going to approach your sales pitch now? You might never know the real results of Starbucks unless you look at their income statement and use it to help you answer questions like these:

- What were the company's sales revenues?
- What types of expenses did it have?
- What was its net profit margin?
- What was its net income and earnings per share?
- How are all of these numbers trending?

These are the questions business leaders have to answer on an almost daily basis. More than just knowing the answers, they are responsible for developing strategies and plans that optimize these metrics to keep the company profitable and growing. It is their primary responsibility to the stakeholders of the company, and the income statement is one way they communicate the results of their strategies and decisions. By the way if you look at Starbucks stock performance after Howard Schultz's comments, he was right!

AKA

The income statement is also referred to as a *statement of earnings*, a *statement of operations*, or more commonly, a *profit and loss statement* or P&L.

PURPOSE AND EQUATION

The purpose of an income statement is to show whether the company made or lost money during the period being reported, usually a quarter or a fiscal year—to show whether a company generated a profit or a loss. This is one reason many companies refer to their income statement as a profit and loss statement (P&L), a sign that it's going to teach us something about the profit driver we explored in chapter 2. But it also reveals important information about the growth driver (chapter 4), because an income statement typically provides data for the current reporting period (quarter or year) and data from the two previous periods. This makes it easy to see the growth in key measures from one period to the next.

Every financial statement is laid out based on a simple formula. The income statement will always start with revenue (the top line), subtract expenses, and end with a calculation of net income or net profit (the bottom line).

Revenue – Expenses = Profit

Think about an income statement like climbing down a ladder. The top rung (top line) represents your sales. Then you'll have a bunch of rungs that represent different costs or expenses. Finally, the bottom rung (bottom line) represents your profit, or how much you made after you subtracted all your expenses. Your family budget follows a similar formula. You earn money from your job and maybe some investments; this is your top line. Then you subtract your mortgage, your car payment, gas, food, entertainment, etc.; these are your expenses. What's left over at the end of the month is your bottom line, and you hope it's not negative. If it is, you start to look for trends, for ways to control your budget, like eating out less to control your food costs.

While a bit more complex, business leaders use the income statement to make equally important decisions to keep sales and profit growing.

As we explore the income statement, I'll first give you what I call my Big-Picture Breakdown so that you can get key information from any income statement in a matter of minutes, and for those interested in more detail, I'll dig in and give you some guidance on a deeper analysis of the numbers that you can get through in about thirty minutes with some practice.

Note: As you walk through the financials in this chapter and the next two, it may be easier for your study to download and print Austin's Cycle Shop financial statements by going to www.seeingthebigpicture. com. You may find that taking notes on the financials will also enhance your understanding.

Austin's Cycle Shop
Consolidated Income Statement
(in thousands, except per-share amounts)

For the year ended December 31	2012	2011	2010	
Total Revenue	$8,300	$7,200	$6,400	← Top line
Cost of Goods Sold	4,600	4,200	3,840	
Gross Profit	3,700	3,000	2,560	
Operating Expenses:				
Research and development	500	440	369	
Sales and marketing	850	730	641	
General and administrative	370	320	270	
Depreciation and amortization	486	328	256	
Total Operating Expenses	2,206	1,818	1,536	
Operating Income	1,494	1,182	1,024	
Interest income	300	200	107	
Interest expense	96	53	58	
Income before provision for income taxes	1,698	1,329	1,073	
Provision for income taxes	611	478	386	
Net Income	$1,087	$851	$687	← Bottom line
Basic earnings per share	$0.27	$0.26	$0.23	
Diluted earnings per share	$0.25	$0.25	$0.22	
Shares used in per-share calculation—basic	4,002	3,275	2,988	
Shares used in per-share calculation—diluted	4,300	3,408	3,112	

BIG PICTURE BREAKDOWN:
THE INCOME STATEMENT IN A MATTER OF MINUTES

What do you want to see when assessing a company through an income statement and only have a couple of minutes? Let's break it down.

Revenue growth year over year: Total revenue (also called sales) is referred to as the top line, because it's at the top of the income statement. You'll want to look at the revenue totals shown for the past three periods. Is revenue increasing? If so, great. If not, this is a big red flag. Steadily decreasing revenue is a sign that the company might be struggling. Next, calculate the rate of growth using the following formula to determine the rate of change:

$$\frac{\text{current year revenue} - \text{previous year revenue}}{\text{previous year revenue}} \times 100 = \text{growth rate \%}$$

Compare the growth rates for the past few years. Even if revenue is heading up each year, a declining rate of growth in revenue might indicate problems with the long-term viability of the company, particularly if the economy and industry have been strong.

Net income growth year over year: Net income, or profit, is referred to as the bottom line of the income statement (even though earnings per share is presented below net income). Has it been increasing over time? Has the rate of growth been steady or improving? If not, compare it to revenue. If revenue is growing, but net income isn't, your expenses are growing faster than your revenue, which may not be good. But some sound business strategies might increase expenses and reduce profit in certain periods, like investing in new product development to make the company more profitable in the future. If profit is declining, do some research to see if company leaders have made those types of investments.

Net profit margin: If you divide the "bottom line" net income by the "top line" total revenue, you have calculated net profit margin. Recall from chapter 2 that net profit margin reveals how much profit is generated by each dollar of revenue. Obviously, you want your revenue to produce as much profit as possible, except when you are reinvesting potential profits into the company as part of a growth strategy.

THE INCOME STATEMENT
IN ABOUT 30 MINUTES

We just covered the income statement in a matter of minutes. If you want to go deeper—maybe you have a big budget meeting with your VP—you should carefully review the following six measures:

- Revenue

- Cost of goods sold

- Gross profit or gross margin

- Operating income

- Net income (profit)

- Earnings per share (EPS)

As I walk you through each of these six measures it's important to remember that different companies will use different terms in their financial statements. If you remember that revenue and sales are essentially synonymous, and that income, earnings, and profit are synonymous as well, it will be easier to read any income statement.

In chapter 7 we discussed the importance of looking at four basic characteristics of a financial measure: amount, trend, ratio, and industry or competitor comparison. While I won't do this for every line item, I will do it for the most important, in this chapter and the next two (note that ratio analysis isn't always possible or necessary). And I would encourage you to do it for any line item that is of particular interest to you.

Let's return to Austin's Cycle Shop to dig into a "real" income statement. Austin's is now seventeen years old and has been a public company for about five years—five good years, in fact. Austin's consolidated income statement, shown on page 124, presents numbers for the years ending December 31, 2012, 2011, and 2010. You see that total revenue is the first item. It is followed by expenses, which are often presented in order of the most *directly* related to operations (cost of goods sold) to the most *indirectly* related to operations (taxes). The bottom line is net income, with an additional line for earnings per share for publicly traded companies.

Keep in mind that the income statement we're using is a bit simplified; most income statements show line items not contained in Austin's. But you don't have to understand every line item to get a very good sense of a company's performance.

Revenue

Revenue is the dollar amount of goods and services sold as a result of your normal business activities. A company's health depends on how well it makes money doing what it normally does—not from extra, nonrecurring activities, such as selling a business unit. Revenue is sometimes referred to as *sales*, *gross revenue*, or *operating revenue*.

The total revenue—the "top line"—is one of the key measures to examine on any income statement. Usually, when a company says that it grew by x or y percent, it's talking about growth in revenues. Austin's has total revenue of $8,300 or $8.3 million for 2012 (remember the numbers are in thousands). This is the money that Austin's makes from the sale of bikes and other goods and services. The revenue received from services—like bike repair—is included in this line item, although some companies might list it separately.

While Austin's Cycle Shop seems to have strong revenue, the proof is really in the comparison. Remember, growth is the key. From 2010 to 2011, Austin's revenues grew more than 12.5 percent, and from 2011 to 2012 its sales grew more than 15.3 percent. Its revenues are trending up, and the rate of revenue growth has *increased*. And if we compare Austin's revenue growth to the sporting goods industry overall, for which sales grew on average about 7 percent annually during the most recent five-year period, the results are even more impressive.

Overall, Austin's revenue numbers provide only positive indicators for the performance of the company.

Cost of Goods Sold

Several categories of expenses are listed after total revenues, but many P&Ls list cost of goods sold (COGS), which is sometimes called *cost of sales*, as the first line item under revenues. As I described in chapter 2, COGS includes the cost of purchasing inventory such as raw materials, costs of product assembly, and other costs directly associated with producing individual products.

Austin's has combined the cost of product sales and services, although some companies may separate the costs out, particularly if they separated them under revenue. Its COGS for 2012 was $4.6 million. You'll notice that, as an accounting practice, none of the numbers in the expense categories are shown as negative (in parentheses). Everyone just knows that *expenses* are *deductions* from revenue.

COGS has increased steadily each year, but that's common when revenue is increasing. What you want to watch out for are increases in COGS as a percent of revenue.

Gross Profit and Gross Margin

Even though, as you may recall from chapter 2, gross profit is an important indicator of profitability and gross profit margin is an important measure for certain industries, such as manufacturers and retailers, few income statements have a line item labeled "gross profit." I've included it on Austin's P&L to keep it simple, but generally, you just have to calculate it. Luckily, it's easily done by subtracting cost of goods sold from the total revenue.

Gross profit = Total revenue – Cost of goods sold

Austin's gross profit for 2012 is $3.7 million (sales of $8.3 million less cost of goods sold of $4.6 million). Gross profit for 2011 was $3 million, and for 2010 it was $2.56 million, showing a nice *upward trend.*

Gross profit margin (gross margin for short) is gross profit as a percent of total revenue. It is an important measure because it indicates how much profit is being generated from your sales before subtracting out overhead and other types of expenses. To some degree, it's a ratio of efficiency and profitability.

To calculate gross margin, you simply divide gross profit by total revenue and multiply by 100:

$$\frac{\text{Gross profit}}{\text{Total Revenue}} \times 100 = \text{Gross Profit Margin \%}$$

For 2012, Austin's gross profit margin or gross margin is:

$$\frac{\text{Gross profit \$3,700}}{\text{Revenue \$8,300}} \times 100 = 45\%$$

A gross profit margin of 45 percent is quite good, particularly compared with the retail bicycle industry average of 37 percent. I find it helpful to write this percentage next to gross profit as I do my analysis. The gross profit margin for 2011 was 42 percent and for 2010 was 40 percent. Gross profit margin was *up* from 2011 to 2012 by 3 percentage points. This is a big improvement, and if you saw this on an income statement, you would want to find out why it improved. For example, was it a one-time occurrence because of a deal the company got on inventory, or will it hold steady in upcoming reporting periods?

Operating Expenses

After the costs of goods sold are subtracted from total revenue, operating expenses are itemized on the income statement. This is one area where you may find dramatic differences from company to company.

For 2012, Austin's first operating expense listed is research and development of $500,000. As its name implies, this is the money spent on researching and developing new products or enhancements to existing products. This is one expense that you want to spend the right amount on: cutting it may impact future sales or profit, and spending too much impacts near-term profit. I like to compare this amount to what the competition is spending. If it's substantially more or less and sales happen to be declining, that is a red flag.

The next line item, which is also fairly straightforward, is sales and marketing of $850,000. This expense could—should—help drive future sales. General and administrative expenses, often referred to simply as G&A or overhead, follow. This line item includes rent, utilities, and salaries of corporate staff, such as finance, HR, and IT personnel. An important note about G&A expenses: They are often targeted when expense reductions are needed because cutting these costs should have less of an impact on sales than cutting R&D or sales and marketing. So keep an eye out for big changes in this line item and do research to find out what they mean.

Depreciation and amortization is the last operating expense on Austin's income statement, and it bears a little more explanation. According to the SEC website, depreciation "takes into account the wear and tear on some assets, such as machinery, tools and furniture, which are used over the long term. Companies spread the cost of these assets over the periods they are used. This process of spreading these costs is called depreciation or amortization [depending on the type of asset]. The 'charge' for using these assets during the period is a fraction of the original cost of the assets." The IRS gives specific guidelines for the number of years different types of assets can be depreciated or amortized.

Higher deductions—expenses—in a given year result in lower taxable net income, and thus lower taxes, which is why reinvesting profits into a business is a tactic company leaders use not only to spur growth, but also to reduce their tax burden.

Operating Income

Once all of the operating expenses have been accounted for, there is enough information to calculate operating income—a *very* important number that shows how much money the company is making from its core operations or basic business activities. Operating income is the profit from core operations—what's left after the cost of goods sold and operating expenses are deducted from revenues, and before subtracting additional expenses that most employees and managers can't control, such as interest and taxes. Operating income for many companies is often referred to as *earnings before interest and taxes*, or EBIT, if there are no unusual expenses in addition to interest and taxes.

Operating income shows how well the company executes its core business functions day to day. Because of this, some analysts, finance professionals, and CEOs see it as a better indicator of profitability than net income. Ideally, this figure should be increasing in dollar amounts each year, as well as increasing in rate of growth year over year. Austin's operating income in the current year was $1.494 million. Growth from 2010 to 2011 was 15 percent and from 2011 to 2012 was 26 percent, an improving trend. Young companies typically grow revenue and operating income faster in the early years than in later years as the business matures. Still, this jump in the rate of growth is quite good.

Operating income or profit as a percent of revenue (operating income divided by revenue, or operating margin) is an important ratio called operating margin. For 2010, 2011, and 2012, Austin's operating margin was 16 percent, 16.4 percent, and 18 percent, respectively. This is a steady improvement in the ratio, indicating that Austin's recent operating costs are growing but not as fast as sales. Some costs stay constant or grow more slowly when volume rises, which improves profits.

Operating margins, like other margins, can vary dramatically from industry to industry and from company to company. For a recent five-year period, the average operating margin for the S&P 500 companies was about 16 percent. Retail stores tend to average less than other industries, so Austin's operating margin is currently very strong. And Austin's recent growth of 26 percent in operating income is significantly above the average growth rate for most companies.

Other Expenses and Income

Nonoperating expenses are those costs that do not relate to the basic operations of the company. Although not listed on Austin's income statement, you may find a line item in this section labeled "nonoperating income or expenses," which could refer to the sale of an asset or business. These incomes or losses would be listed in this section because they are not part of the company's core business. Moving to the next line item, Austin's had interest income of $300,000 in 2012, which is the interest earned on its cash and investments. We then find an interest expense of $96,000. This is the interest Austin's paid on its debt for the year. You may wonder why companies borrow money when they seem to have plenty of cash on hand. There are several reasons, including very cheap borrowing rates and the desire to keep plenty of cash on hand for future investments for growth. The last expense is the provision for income taxes in the amount of $611,000. This includes taxes paid and taxes accrued (owed) but not yet paid.

Net Income or Net Earnings—The Bottom Line

How much net income (profit) did Austin's make after all expenses were paid and all revenue was accounted for? This is the bottom line, and in many ways is the most important figure on the income statement. Austin's net income for 2012 was $1.087 million. It was positive, so that's a strong starting point. Better than that, net income has increased each year. And the *rate* of growth improved from 24 percent from 2010 to 2011, to 28 percent from 2011 to 2012. Good news for the company, but why did it occur? If you worked for Austin's Cycle Shop, this is a question you should ask, and we will answer it next.

Net income as a percent of total revenue is called *net margin* or *net profit margin* (net income divided by revenue, or "bottom line" divided by "top line"), as we discussed in chapter 2. Austin's net profit margins (rounded) were 11 percent for 2010, 12 percent for 2011, and 13 percent for 2012 (this is an important percentage you may want to write on the income statement next to net income). Austin has been able to contain the rate of growth of the company's costs to be *less* than the rate of growth of its revenue—that's good. If the net profit margin were *decreasing*, it would mean that sales were growing at a rate less than costs—that wouldn't be so good. The S&P 500 average net profit margin for the last five years is around 11 percent, so Austin's has been able to survive and thrive. Remember that companies with unique offerings, like Apple, typically have higher margins, while companies like Walmart, which sell commodities, have lower than average profit margins. If you aren't unique, you better be cheap!

Earnings Per Share

For public companies, income statements will include some final entries that calculate the earnings (profit) generated per share of common stock outstanding—the EPS. This may be the most important measure in determining a company's share price. Why? Because for any investment, the more profit it generates the more valuable it is. A company that is able to earn more per each share of stock over time will see its stock price go up; as we discussed in chapter 6, this is important to employees, leaders, and shareholders. Earnings per share are calculated by dividing the net income by the average number of shares of common stock outstanding during the year or period:

$$\text{Earnings Per Share (EPS)} = \frac{\text{Net Income}}{\text{Shares of Common Stock}}$$

There are two ways to present earnings per share. Basic EPS uses the number of currently outstanding shares of common stock as the denominator; Austin's basic EPS for 2012 is $0.27. Diluted EPS adds to the outstanding common stock the number of shares that would be outstanding if all stock options of value—options to purchase stock, usually at a stated price, granted to employees and other stakeholders—were exercised. Austin had 298,000 stock options outstanding in 2012 (4,300,000 diluted shares minus 4,002,000 basic shares). Therefore, Austin's diluted EPS for 2012 is $.25, which is no change from 2011, but an increase from 2010 ($.22), a positive trend. Most analysts use fully diluted EPS for their apples-to-apples comparisons, so assume *fully diluted* when you read about EPS in the media or elsewhere.

One last point: Over time the number of shares outstanding might change, and therefore EPS might change with the same net income. Austin and his board of directors can choose to issue more shares of stock to raise more money; give stock options to employees; or buy back shares of stock and "retire" them. Note that they have increased the average number of common shares outstanding each year from 2010 to 2012. This explains why net income increased 28 percent from 2011 to 2012, while EPS remained flat.

You can improve your company's income statement by helping to increase revenue or reduce expenses, which creates more profit. If you are part of a public company, your contribution to increasing net profit, or earnings, will also increase EPS. By helping to increase revenue or decrease expenses, you are helping to increase your stock price! The ideas in chapter 2 for what you can do specifically to impact profit apply to the income statement, too.

INSIGHTS INTO THE INCOME STATEMENT

- The income statement measures profitability.

- The income statement formula is Revenue – Expenses = Profit (Net Income). It shows top-line revenue (sales), deducts all expenses, and shows bottom-line net income or profit.

- The income statement is a financial "motion picture" showing company performance over a period of time, such as a month, quarter, or fiscal year.

- The income statement is also referred to as the *statement of operations, statement of earnings, the profit and loss statement*, or the *P&L*.

- Key measures to watch on an income statement are total revenue, gross profit, operating income, net income, and earnings per share (for public companies).

- Net profit margin is your "bottom line" net income or earnings as a percent of total revenues or sales.

- Everything you do to impact profit—primarily increasing sales or reducing expenses, including cost of goods sold—influences the bottom line of your income statement.

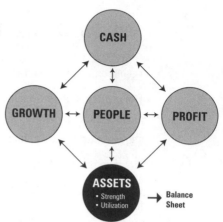

Chapter 9

BALANCE SHEET: TRACKING ASSETS

There are men who can write poetry,
and there are men who can read balance sheets.
The men who can read balance sheets cannot write.
—Henry R. Luce

When Lehman Brothers declared bankruptcy on September 15, 2008, it had assets of about $691 billion, making it the largest bankruptcy filing in history. The second largest happened just eleven days later when Washington Mutual, with $328 billion in assets, went under and was purchased by Chase. These two bankruptcies, along with the many that followed, were significant contributors to the Great Recession. Warren Buffett, once said, "It's only when the tide goes out that you learn who's been swimming naked," meaning companies are able to hide unhealthy risk when times are good, but are quickly exposed during economic downturns.

How prepared is your company to weather the storms of business or take advantage of a major opportunity? If there were a significant downturn in your market or the economy, a severe credit crisis, another 9/11, or an unforeseen opportunity to make a major acquisition, would your company be capable of performing? What reserves or staying power do you have? These are the questions a balance sheet can answer.

PURPOSE AND EQUATION

The balance sheet provides information on assets, liabilities, and equity—factors of your asset strength and, along with the income statement, indicators of how effectively your assets are being utilized to produce a return.

Just like the income statement, the balance sheet follows a basic equation:

$$\text{Assets} - \text{Liabilities} = \text{Equity}$$

or

$$\text{Assets} = \text{Liabilities} + \text{Equity}$$

Recall from chapter 3 that your assets are the resources and items you *own* that have economic value, such as cash, accounts receivable, buildings, equipment, and other things you use to produce revenue or income. Liabilities are debts you *owe*, such as bank loans, accounts payable, mortgage loans, etc. Equity (stockholders' equity or net assets) is what the owners (stockholders) would have left over after selling all of the assets and paying off all the liabilities.

Asset strength is a strong indicator of overall financial health. Why? Because a company can rely on its assets in times of trouble. Suppose you, as an individual, have plenty of cash in savings, investments of different types, good equity in your home (all assets), and very little debt. You're more likely to survive financially during a downturn or loss of job, aren't you? The same principle is true of companies.

Remember, asset strength is primarily measured in terms of liquidity—how much cash and cash equivalents are available or could be generated quickly by selling assets—and the relationship of liabilities to assets and equity. You want your assets to be greater than your liabilities, and the more equity you have, the less risk you carry. If your company has a loan of $1 million to be repaid in ninety days, and it has $5 million of cash or assets that can be turned into cash within ninety days, it's in good shape. But if it's the reverse—well, good luck!

Let's explore the relationship between assets, liabilities, and equity a bit more before we dive into the balance sheet.

WHY THE BALANCE SHEET BALANCES AND WHY MORE EQUITY EQUALS LESS RISK

Assets *must* equal liabilities plus equity; let's explore why.

Suppose you want to purchase a home (asset) and the price is $200,000. Where do you get the money to buy it? You take out an 80 percent mortgage loan (liability) for $160,000 and make a down payment of $40,000 (equity). The capital you used to buy your home—your $160,000 liability (mortgage loan)—plus your $40,000 equity (cash down payment) equals $200,000, the price of your asset (home). Now suppose you get very lucky and within six months of purchasing the home the market goes up and your home is now worth $50,000 more. You haven't paid down the principal portion of the mortgage loan much, so now your $250,000 asset equals your $160,000 liability plus your $90,000 ($40,000 + $50,000) equity. The $50,000 jump in value increased your equity in the house.

This is exactly how a balance sheet for a company works. The balance sheet shows your company's assets and the sources of capital (cash) used to acquire or fund those assets. The balance sheet "balances" because it shows that the money to purchase your assets came from (or balances with) the total of what you borrowed (liabilities) plus what you earned or contributed from your own pocket (equity).

The home example is also a good example of why asset strength and strong equity are equated with less risk. Let's say that instead of increasing in value, your home value dropped by $50,000. Now your $150,000 home would equal your $160,000 liability plus $10,000 in negative equity. That's what you would have to pay the bank if you sold your home today, in order to maintain good credit with the bank. If you are still able to make your loan payments, then negative equity may not be a problem. However, if you had more equity from the start to offset the liability of the loan, a drop of $50,000 wouldn't have resulted in negative equity. Or if you had other assets, such as $15,000 in the bank, covering the negative equity in your home wouldn't be a problem. If you didn't have assets to cover your negative equity, that would make you a risky borrower.

This is why banks, investors, and analysts review the balance sheet closely to determine how risky it is to loan money to, invest in, or buy stock in a company. They want to see enough asset strength to cover all of the eventualities that businesses are exposed to every day, such as a downturn in the market or the failure of a new product.

A significant contributor to the credit crisis that began in 2007 was financial institutions, lowering their lending standards and accepting riskier loans, with borrowers investing very little of their own money, say 5 percent. As the value of homes dropped, many lost all of their equity (in 2011 about one in seven homes was underwater) and their incentive to keep making payments. And as loans for banks went south, they had less money to lend to others, including businesses.

To help you understand how to quickly get key indicators of your company's financial strength from the balance sheet, I've presented the Big Picture Breakdown. If you're ready for a more in-depth look at the balance sheet, read through the rest of the chapter, too.

Austin's Cycle Shop
Consolidated Balance Sheet
(in thousands, except per-share amounts)

As of December 31	2012	2011
Assets		
Current Assets:		
Cash and cash equivalents	$827	$580
Short-term investments	1,189	1,157
Accounts receivable	1,242	1,303
Inventories	652	362
Prepaid expenses and other current assets	705	412
Total Current Assets	**4,615**	**3,814**
Long-term investments	3,202	2,017
Property and equipment, net	2,913	1,969
Goodwill and other intangibles	10	
Other assets	1,787	1,162
Total Assets	**12,527**	**$8,962**
Liabilities and Shareholders' Equity		
Current Liabilities:		
Accounts payable	$361	$250
Income taxes payable	576	411
Accrued payroll and related expenses	571	392
Other accrued liabilities	750	728
Total Current Liabilities	**2,258**	**1,781**
Long-term debt	343	143
Total Liabilities	**2,601**	**1,924**
Shareholders' Equity:		
Common stock and additional paid-in capital, $0.001 par value 5,400 shares authorized: 4,002 shares issued and outstanding in 2012 and 3,210 shares in 2011, 198 options outstanding	5,011	3,210
Retained earnings	4,915	3,828
Total Shareholders' Equity	**9,926**	**7,038**
Total Liabilities and Shareholders' Equity	**$12,527**	**$8,962**

BIG PICTURE BREAKDOWN:
THE BALANCE SHEET IN A MATTER OF MINUTES

What do you want to see when assessing a company through a balance sheet and only have a couple of minutes? Let's break it down for a quick analysis.

Cash position: Recall from chapter 1 that a company's cash position is the amount listed for "cash and cash equivalents"—how much it has on hand or in accessible accounts at any point in time. A company should have a strong cash position on its balance sheet so that it can weather tough times or take advantage of opportunities. The worse the economy or the industry is doing, the more cash you want to see on hand.

Cash position change: How has the cash position changed year over year or quarter over quarter? If it has increased, that may be a good thing—unless the company is holding on to too much cash (cash earns a pretty lousy return) or isn't investing in the growth of the company. If it has decreased, why? Has the company used cash for a big investment for future growth? Or have revenue and profits been dropping, forcing the company to dig into its cash to keep the doors open?

Equity ratio: The equity ratio is total shareholders' equity divided by total assets, expressed as a percentage:

$$\frac{\text{Shareholders' equity}}{\text{Total assets}} \times 100 = \text{Equity ratio}$$

A high or strong equity ratio means that more of the total assets are financed by shareholders' or owners' equity than by liabilities, or debts. Banks tend to have lower ratios, hi-tech companies higher. A higher ratio means that a company has more equity to borrow against if it needed to (the company is a good credit risk), and the ability to borrow money is an important factor in the potential growth of a company.

Return on Assets (ROA): ROA measures the profit generated on the company's assets. The purpose of assets is to earn a return for the stakeholders, and profit is the best form of return. The equation is:

$$\frac{\text{Net Income}}{\text{Total assets}} \times 100 = \text{Return on Assets (ROA)}$$

The higher the percentage, the better. The S&P 500 average is typically about 7 percent.

THE BALANCE SHEET IN ABOUT 30 MINUTES

A balance sheet is a snapshot, providing a financial picture of your company on a specific date—usually the last day of a month, quarter, or fiscal year. Accounting standards require that at least two periods be shown. If you look at the balance sheet for Austin's Cycle Shop, you'll see information as of December 31, 2012, and December 31, 2011.

The most important line items on any balance sheet, and the ones we'll fully analyze in the following pages, are:

- Current assets, particularly cash and cash equivalents
- Total assets
- Current liabilities
- Total liabilities
- Shareholders' equity

Current Assets

A balance sheet always lists assets beginning with the most liquid—the current assets. Current assets are those the company expects to convert to cash within twelve months. (Note that I'm using guidelines for U.S.-based companies. Businesses based outside of the United States might have different formats.)

It's important to note that the dollar amount of assets included on the balance sheet is typically the original cost of the asset less any accumulated depreciation. Inventories are valued at either cost or market value, whichever is lower. These accounting rules guard against inflating the value of assets, but they might also lead to understating the true value of a company. For example, a company that purchased a building thirty years ago might show no value for the building on its balance sheet because the asset has been entirely depreciated ("written off") over this period. However, the building might still be in good condition and valuable if sold—possibly worth even more than its original cost.

Corporate raiders evaluate companies based on the *fair market value* of its assets—*not* the dollar amount on their balance sheet (its book value).

Cash is the most liquid asset, so is listed first within current assets. It includes funds in banks and other financial accounts as well as cash equivalents that are almost as liquid as cash, such as an interest in a money market fund. The reason this is such an important line item, as discussed in chapter 1, is because it reflects a company's flexibility, or its ability to take advantage of opportunities in the marketplace, invest in new products, or survive through downturns.

Obviously, we want to see that a company has enough cash to cover its immediate expenses and still have a surplus for emergencies. As we discussed in chapter 1, there is no magic number. It varies from company to company and industry to industry. Retailers, like Target, generally carry less cash compared to large technology companies like Cisco, Google, and Apple, which carry much more. If the amount of cash held is too high, you might ask whether the company is holding too much cash—cash that it could be investing to earn a higher return elsewhere or that it could use to pay dividends to investors, if it's public. Austin's showed cash and cash equivalents of $827,000 for 2012.

We generally want to see the amount of cash increasing over time, or at least increasing as revenue and earnings are increasing. However, a company may make a strategic decision to use cash to invest in an opportunity, pay dividends to shareholders, or even pay bonuses to employees. If there is a drop in cash from period to period, you should ask the question "How was that cash used?" which can be answered by reviewing the statement of cash flows, as we'll discuss in the next chapter. Austin's cash balance did grow from $580,000 to $827,000, a 43 percent increase year over year. You may remember that Austin's net income or profit grew by 28 percent in the same period (as shown on the income statement), so the increase in cash is not surprising.

After cash, companies itemize other current, but slightly less liquid, assets. Short-term investments, such as securities like stocks and bonds that will mature within one year, were $1.189 million for Austin's. If a company has this line item on its balance sheet, it has a strong enough cash position that it can invest some of that cash to generate a higher return without risking its financial security.

Companies identify accounts receivable, money due from customers who have purchased on credit, on their balance sheet. Austin's accounts receivable was $1.242 million in 2012, decreasing from $1.303 in 2011, even though sales increased. That is actually a good sign, because it shows that the company is collecting cash faster and can use that collected money sooner to invest in income-producing assets.

The next line item is inventory of $652,000 and reflects the actual costs of the inventory, such as raw materials, the labor, and the manufacturing overhead involved in creating the inventory. Austin's inventory grew 80 percent—from $362,000 to $652,000—which is a faster growth rate than its sales, a potential red flag. Austin's shouldn't build up more inventory than it needs, as this ties up cash, adds storage costs, and increases the risk of outdated product. A buildup of inventory could be justified if Austin's is planning for a big sales push or increase in demand with new store openings.

Prepaid expenses is money your company has paid to another entity, which can be considered an asset until the products or services paid for have been delivered. For example, companies may pay their insurance premiums in January and have the benefit (an asset) of being covered for the next six months. Austin's prepaid expenses and other current assets increased from $412,000 in 2011 to $705,000 in 2012. Part of this may have been due to down payments on inventory it has yet to receive. Ideally, a company would prepay expenses as little as possible, unless it can obtain good discounts, so that it can keep its cash longer.

Once all the current assets are listed, they are totaled, and the total is a good indicator of liquidity, particularly when compared to current liabilities (I'll discuss the current ratio when we review liabilities). Austin's had total current assets of $4.615 million in 2012.

Total Assets

After the total current assets line, the balance sheet presents assets that are *fixed* or *long-term* in nature. Companies don't intend to turn these assets into cash in the next twelve months. For example, Austin's long-term investments of $3.202 million differ from investments in the current asset section because the company intends to hold them for more than one year. A company sitting on more cash than it needs in the short term will look for ways to invest it for a higher return through long-term assets.

Austin's property, plant, and equipment amount of $2.913 million represents the cost of these assets, less the total depreciation that has been booked for them (refer to chapter 8 for a review of depreciation). Austin's increase of nearly $1 million in property, plant, and equipment is in line with the growth strategy for the business.

A curious asset you may see on some balance sheets is goodwill. Goodwill has nothing to do with how well liked a company is or what good deeds it has done. It is the difference between how much a company pays to acquire another company and the value of the acquired company's tangible assets. So goodwill accounts for the value of the intangible assets that were acquired. When P&G bought Gillette (the razor company), much of the value it acquired was not property, plant, and equipment but intangibles like the Gillette brand name, supplier relationships, and the people who were part of Gillette. Austin's Cycle Shop purchased a small supplier that had goodwill and other intangible assets that were worth about $10,000 to Austin's. Austin's wasn't simply buying the fixed assets from this supplier; it also purchased the supplier's contacts, brand strength, and employee expertise, all of which added value to what Austin's was buying. Goodwill stays on the books forever, unless there is a reason to reduce the value. For example, if all of the employees left and sales dropped, the value of the acquisition would drop, and that would be reflected in the goodwill line item. And if

Austin's decided to later sell the supplier's business, the goodwill would be taken off of the balance sheet.

"Other assets" of $1.787 million is the last asset listed on Austin's balance sheet, and it represents the value of noncash assets that are longer term, such as prepaid expenses, accounts receivable, and notes due. You'll notice this line item is growing, and faster than Austin's sales. One of Austin's strategies to boost sales and profits is to offer financing to its bicycle and motorized scooter customers for up to two years. Since this is money owed to Austin's, it is listed as an asset. If much of the growth in this line item is due to Austin's financing more of its sales, Austin's could see a boost in profits, since collecting interest makes financing a profitable business as a result of the interest paid. Of course, this increases Austin's risk, too. Some customers may default on their loans. And financing affects cash flow because the company doesn't receive the cash when it sells a bicycle on credit. Boosting sales by offering credit is a strategy Austin's leaders will want to carefully monitor.

With all assets listed, you can calculate total assets. This line item is important because it represents the foundation the company is building to support its future growth; it is a core component of asset strength and liquidity. In 2012, Austin's had total assets of $12.527 million, which grew from $8.962 million the previous year, a substantial 40 percent increase. Retailers might normally grow total assets at 6 to 10 percent per year, so Austin's asset growth of more than 40 percent is spectacular. Clearly Austin is setting the company up for more sales growth and increased profitability going forward. He is purchasing companies, investing in fixed assets, and growing the cash position.

Other than growth, when reviewing total assets it's helpful to calculate the return on assets (ROA), which was mentioned in the Big Picture Breakdown on page 141 as one of the most important ratios associated with the balance sheet. It reflects asset utilization and organizational efficiency because it tells us how much profit is generated for each dollar invested in assets. Return on assets is calculated as net income divided by total assets. From Austin's income statement in the previous chapter, we know that its net income for 2012 was $1.087 million. That gives it an ROA of 8.7 percent; for every $100 of assets, the company is currently earning $8.70. That's a good ROA, surpassing the average ROA for most industries of about 7 percent and for Austin's industry of about 5 percent. (ROAs have been pushed down in recent years by the recession, but the average five-year ROA for software companies is about 13 percent and for auto companies is about 4 percent.) Austin's ROA in 2011 was a bit higher at 9.5 percent. While Austin's return on assets dropped 0.8 percent in the past year, that is nothing to panic over—but it is a trend to watch. A company should be striving to improve its ROA over time, using its assets more and more efficiently to generate profit. However, it's not uncommon to see a drop in ROA in companies that are focused on growth. They may invest in a number of assets to prepare for growth, but it may take time for those assets to generate the profit expected. For instance, Austin's purchased a company this year, and acquisitions can be notoriously slow at proving their worth.

Current Liabilities

Liabilities—obligations we have to others—are used to finance and grow operations, and are thus necessary in most companies. However, accumulating too many liabilities, particularly in relation to assets or equity, can be a sign that a company is becoming too leveraged or less liquid, or that profits may begin to suffer. More liabilities usually mean greater interest payments, and interest payments impact the bottom line. A significant factor in the downgrade of the U.S. government's credit rating in 2011 was the accumulation of too much liability (debt).

Because liabilities are paid or settled over time, they are listed in order of those due the soonest (current liabilities, such as trade accounts payable) to those due latest (such as long-term debt or mortgage loan notes). As we go through Austin's liabilities you will notice that each line item has increased in the past year, and as you can guess, this is due to Austin's strategy for growth. Also, remember that a good cash strategy is to pay liabilities as slowly as possible without incurring penalties or damaging supplier relationships.

Current liabilities are liabilities due to be paid within twelve months. As shown on Austin's balance sheet, current liabilities begin with accounts payable of $361,000—the total of invoices the company has in hand but has not yet paid. This would include expenses for utilities, rents, inventory purchased, etc. Next, income taxes payable of $576,000 are taxes that are owed but have not yet been paid. For example, a company paying taxes on a quarterly basis will accrue taxes for three months before making payment. "Accrued payroll and related expenses" refers to money that is owed to employees but has not yet been paid. This does not mean that Austin's is holding out on its employees' paychecks! The $571,000 in 2012 may be related to commissions, bonuses, or benefits that are earned over time and paid at the end of the quarter or year. Other accrued liabilities of $750,000 is the catchall for liabilities that do not fit into the above line items, such as retirement obligations.

It is preferable for current liabilities to be less than current assets. Austin's current liabilities for the 2012 were $2.258 million, less than the current assets of $4.615 million—a good sign. Austin's current liabilities grew 27 percent in the last two years, a substantial increase, particularly considering that current assets grew by only 21 percent. This is a bit of a red flag. Austin's has been pushing for growth, and that typically results in a jump in liabilities.

A critical question to ask when reviewing current liabilities is "Are there enough current assets to pay for all the current liabilities?" The current ratio, one of the most important measures of liquidity, can help you answer this question. The *current ratio* is simply current assets divided by current liabilities. The higher the current ratio, the more liquid and secure a company is, because it is more able to pay off its current liabilities. If the current ratio is greater than 1, the company has more current assets than current liabilities. If it's less than 1, the company has more current liabilities than current assets and would be unable to pay off its current liabilities if they suddenly came due unless it borrowed money or sold an asset. Austin's current ratio for 2012 was about 2.0 and tells us that for every dollar it will owe in the next year, it should have about 2 dollars coming in. Although the current ratio dropped slightly from 2.1 in 2011, it compares very favorably with many retailers. By current-ratio analysis alone, Austin's Cycle Shop is more conservatively structured than either Walmart or Target. The average company today has a current ratio of about 1.1.

Total Liabilities

Once the current liabilities are tallied, the long-term liabilities are listed. These are financial obligations that extend beyond twelve months. Austin's long-term debt of $343,000 in 2012 is up from $143,000 in 2011, but since Austin's has a strong equity position, as we will see shortly, this does not raise a concern. The company has financed some of its growth by borrowing, which is a good way to fund growth, especially when interest rates are low. Many companies itemize their long-term debts, including line items for mortgage loans, retiree benefits, long-term lease obligations (for office space, equipment, or other assets), and notes or bonds issued that are due to be paid beyond twelve months.

Once all liabilities are listed, they can be tallied to determine *total liabilities*, an important line item because it reflects the total debt of the company, which can be compared with total assets or equity. In 2012, Austin's had total liabilities of $2.601 million, which grew a substantial 35 percent (from $1.924 million) over the previous year. This was less than the total asset increase of 40 percent, so the company is becoming slightly less leveraged.

To get some context for total liabilities, let's look at the debt ratio, a comparison of total liabilities to total assets (total liabilities divided by total assets). Austin's debt ratio has been about 0.21 for the past two years, which means that about 21 percent of its asset value is financed through debt. This is quite low, a good sign of financial strength. Many companies, including retailers, have debt ratios that are much higher, meaning they incur a fair amount of debt to acquire their assets.

Shareholders' Equity

Shareholders' equity is the third major category after assets and liabilities. It is sometimes called *stockholders' equity*, or *partners' capital* if the business is a privately held partnership and is the difference between total assets and total liabilities.

There are a few items that may be included under stockholders' equity, particularly for public companies. The first is common stock and additional paid-in capital. When stock is first issued, it is valued at a nominal figure, a *par value* such as $0.01 (1 cent) per share. When the stock is purchased by investors, its price is always substantially more than par value. The additional amount paid by investors over the par value per share is known as additional paid-in capital. For Austin's Cycle Shop, equity coming from stock (actual cash paid for the stock when it was issued) was $5.011 million in 2012. The number of shares of common stock issued and outstanding are identified on the balance sheet as well. You can see from 2011 to 2012 that the number of shares issued and outstanding increased from 3,210,000 to 4,002,000, which means that Austin's issued more stock. As a result, additional paid-in capital, or cash generated from issuing stock, increased from $3.210 million to $5.011 million.

We just discussed how equity is built in a company through issuing stock to shareholders. The other important way to build equity is through a company's profits. When a company shows a profit or loss on its income statement, this amount (less dividends distributed to shareholders) is added (profits) or subtracted (losses) to the retained earnings category on the balance sheet. If it were not, assets would not balance with liabilities and equity. Profits and losses accumulate over the years in retained earnings. So retained earnings is a reflection of the accumulated profits that have not been paid out as a dividend. As earnings are retained in the company, the assets grow. As you can see, Austin's retained earnings grew by $1.087 million from 2011 to 2012, which is the exact amount of net income shown on the income statement in

2012. Since Austin's is not paying a dividend, all of its 2012 net income or profit was retained in the company and therefore increased the company's shareholders' equity.

In 2012, Austin's had shareholders' equity of $9.926 million, a growth rate of a substantial 41 percent over 2011 (from $7.038 million). This is slightly more than its total asset increase of 40 percent because its liabilities grew at a slower rate of 35 percent.

Shareholders' equity is used to calculate a number of ratios. The one that I mentioned in the Big Picture Breakdown at the beginning of this chapter is the equity ratio, which measures equity as a percentage of assets. For Austin's Cycle Shop, this ratio was 79 percent in 2012 and slightly less in 2011. This suggests that the company has a lot of equity to borrow against if it needs to raise cash. The average equity ratio varies greatly by industry, with banks generally below 10 percent and tech companies often over 50 percent. With the average company at around 25 percent, Austin's ratio is very strong.

Another important ratio related to shareholders' equity is the debt-to-equity ratio, which is calculated as total liabilities divided by shareholders' equity. While good companies can have liabilities equal to two or three times the amount of equity, this relationship is important to consider. A higher percentage of equity or assets in relationship to liabilities indicates greater financial strength. The debt-to-equity ratio indicates how "leveraged" a company is, meaning how much it has relied on debt to fund its investments, and therefore its growth. A high debt-to-equity ratio means that it has relied more heavily on debt.

What does this mean? Well, with debt come interest expenses, and the more debt, the more interest. So if a company is heavily leveraged, meaning it is primarily using debt to fund its investments, its earnings may be affected over time by interest payments, which impact the bottom line. If times get bad, a highly leveraged company might go under, which happened to many companies in 2008 and 2009. That said, debt is not a bad thing. Most companies need it to grow. And debt can be less costly than other ways of raising capital because, for one, interest payments are tax deductible (they lessen the amount of income on which a company has to pay taxes).

Austin's debt-to-equity ratio is 0.26 ($.26 of debt to $1 of equity; it can also be written as .26:1 or 26 percent) for 2012 and 0.27 for 2011. That's quite low. Most companies try to be in the 0.5-to-1.5 range, but this can vary by industry.

The last line on the balance sheet is *total liabilities and shareholders' equity*. And as you now know, it always equals, or "balances" with, total assets.

What can you do to make a positive impact on the balance sheet of your company?

You can help reduce or eliminate nonproducing assets and acquire more effective assets in the future—for example, keeping inventories down without impairing sales. You can make better use of or conserve cash. You can negotiate better terms on credit and debt. And you can work to improve profitability using the assets you already have.

 INSIGHTS INTO THE BALANCE SHEET

- The balance sheet measures financial strength, especially your company's liquidity and ratios of liabilities (debt) to equity and assets.

- The balance sheet formula is Assets = Liabilities + Equity. This financial statement presents assets first, then liabilities, followed by shareholders' equity.

- The balance sheet must balance the amount of assets with the source of funds to acquire them: liabilities (debt) coming from creditors plus equity coming from the owners.

- The balance sheet is a financial snapshot taken at the end of a month, quarter, or fiscal year.

- Key measures to look for include cash, current assets, total assets, current liabilities, total liabilities, and shareholders' equity.

- Assets are listed beginning with those most liquid through those least liquid. Current assets are those that should be converted to cash within twelve months.

- Net income from the income statement divided by the total assets on the balance sheet is a measure of your company's overall productivity, called return on assets (ROA).

- Liabilities are in order of those due first through those due latest. Current liabilities are those coming due within twelve months.

- The current ratio, which is current assets divided by current liabilities, is a key indicator of liquidity.

- Shareholders' equity is equal to assets minus liabilities and is gener ated by shareholders investing in and profits retained by the company.

- The debt-to-equity ratio indicates how much debt is used to finance the growth of the company over time.

- Everything you do to impact cash, profits, and assets influences your balance sheet.

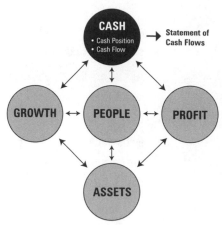

Chapter 10

STATEMENT OF CASH FLOWS

Cash flow is more important than profit.
—*Peter Drucker*

Do you remember when you were in college and in the third week of a month, you would run out of money? So you would make that dreaded call to Mom and Dad. And when you told them you had run out of money, what was the first question they asked? I'm betting it was "What did you do with your money?" Answering that type of question is the purpose of the statement of cash flows. It shows where you got the money, where you spent it, and what you had left over. Of course, this is probably something you wouldn't have wanted to send to your parents. Seeing a hefty sum spent at the local pub as a line item probably wouldn't have made them rush to send you more cash.

In many ways, it's appropriate that we began this book discussing cash and now approach the end by addressing the same topic. Cash flow is that important. Without strong cash flow, a company will quickly die. With it, a company can weather almost any storm. Henry Fudge, owner of Fudge Family Farms, a highly regarded pork producer, learned this lesson the hard way, as he explained to Craig Rogers in his column "Chefs with Issues: Five Sustainable Lessons from a Family Farm" (CNN.com,

June 2, 2011). To grow his business, he entered into a relationship with a wholesaler, who agreed to buy Henry's prime cuts. But that left Henry with too much inventory of "off cuts." Whole animal usage is critical to farms that raise and sell protein animals. Holding on to inventory that he had to invest substantial resources to raise and slaughter limited the cash flow he should have been generating from that product. Although Henry's total revenue initially grew through sales of his premium pork, his profit and cash flow by comparison plummeted, becoming a major contributor to the eventual demise of his business.

AKA

The statement of cash flows is also referred to as the *cash flow statement* and the *sources and uses of cash statement*.

PURPOSE AND EQUATION

The *statement of cash flows* (or the cash flow statement) measures the amount of cash your company generates and uses during a particular reporting period (usually a quarter or a fiscal year), including where it comes from and where it goes. It provides important information about a company's ability to generate cash, pay its debts, make acquisitions, survive market downturns, invest in growth, pay dividends, buy back stock, and otherwise exercise its financial strength.

While the income statement and balance sheet reveal important information about a company, you can't tell from them how much cash your company generated during the reporting period or how much cash was generated from normal operations in contrast to investing and financing activities, the three categories of activities we discussed in chapter 1. This information is just as important as profit or equity when you are trying to assess the health of your company and how you can help it grow. Providing this information is the purpose of the statement of cash flows.

The basic equation for the statement of cash flows is:

Cash from operating activities

+/- Cash from investing activities

+/- Cash from financing activities

= Net increase (or decrease) in cash and equivalents.

Austin's Cycle Shop
Consolidated Statement of Cash Flows
(in thousands, except per-share amounts)

For the year ended December 31	2012	2011	2010
Cash flows from operating activities:			
Net Income	$1,087	$851	$687
Adjustments to reconcile net income to net cash provided by operating activities:			
Depreciation and amortization	486	328	256
Change in operating assets and liabilities:			
Accounts receivable	61	(166)	56
Inventories	(290)	(266)	(205)
Prepaid expenses and other current assets	(293)	22	10
Accounts payable	111	28	15
Income taxes payable	165	154	75
Accrued payroll and related expenses	179	127	63
Other accrued liabilities	22	954	304
Net Cash Provided by Operating Activities	1,528	2,032	1,261
Cash flows from investing activities:			
Capital expenditures	(1,410)	(417)	(389)
Purchases of investments	(1,217)	(1,820)	(1,192)
Other asset purchases	(655)		
Net Cash Used in Investing Activities	(3,282)	(2,237)	(1,581)
Cash flows from financing activities:			
Issuance of common stock	1,801	489	420
Common stock repurchases			
Increase (payment) in long-term debt	200	(10)	0
Net Cash Provided by Financing Activities	2,001	479	420
Net increase in cash and equivalents	247	274	100
Cash and equivalents, beginning of year	580	306	206
Cash and Cash Equivalents, end of year	**$827**	**$580**	**$306**

BIG PICTURE BREAKDOWN:
THE STATEMENT OF CASH FLOWS
IN A MATTER OF MINUTES

If you only have a couple of minutes to review the statement of cash flows, you can still learn a lot about a company:

Cash from operating activities: On the statement of cash flows, look for the line item "net cash provided by operating activities." The dollar amount for this line item had better be positive, unless the company is new and is spending cash to get started. For a mature company, negative cash flow is a very bad omen, and a company with negative cash flow over time is unlikely to survive. This is the most important number on the statement of cash flows!

Growth in cash from operating activities: Ideally, you want the cash provided by operating activities (cash flow) for a company to increase year over year. This means the core business is generating more cash as the company grows, operations are becoming more efficient, and leaders have a better understanding of what resources they need and when. That said, there could be a sound business reason why the number would decline from one period to the next. When cash generated goes down—or up—significantly from one period to the next, this is a red flag that should prompt you to ask, "Why?"

Cash used in (provided by) investing activities: I prefer to see a negative number here, because it indicates a company is investing in assets. Investing in assets is important in order to both maintain existing assets and to acquire new assets needed to support growth.

Cash provided by (used in) financing activities: A positive number for this line item means the company is borrowing money or issuing stock. A negative number means the company is using cash to reduce debt and/or provide value to shareholders.

THE STATEMENT OF CASH FLOWS, IN ABOUT 30 MINUTES

In the cash flow statement, the entries show cash flowing *into* and *out of* the business for operating, investing, and financing activities; the total amount of cash generated from all of the activities; and the cash position. Positive numbers mean *a source of cash* for the business, and negative numbers mean cash *used* by the business. (Note that negative numbers are shown in parentheses. Negative numbers do not mean a loss—just that cash was used for a certain purpose rather than *received*.) For this reason, some finance people will refer to this statement as a Sources and Uses of Cash Statement. The cash flow statement includes numbers from the three most recent reporting periods, making it easy to see changes and trends.

The most important items on this financial report are

- Net cash provided (or used) by operating activities
- Net cash provided (or used) by investing activities
- Net cash provided (or used) by financing activities
- Net change in cash and cash equivalents

Let's look at Austin's cash flow statement to explore how the numbers reveal important details about the business.

Cash Provided (or Used) by Operating Activities

A review of a cash flow statement always begins with determining cash flow from operations, because cash generated from normal business operations, specifically related to the sale of its products or services, is the most important source of cash. To reach a calculation of cash flow from operations, the statement of cash flows begins with net income and makes adjustments to show how cash flowed into and out of the company.

You'll notice that the *first line* of Austin's statement of cash flows is the *bottom line* from the income statement, and both have the same label: net income. Austin's net income for the most recent year was $1.087 million. For Austin's, and any larger organization, net income is an accrual-based number—meaning it is based on the revenues and expenses booked or recorded in a particular period as a result of sales in that period. The company may receive cash from that booked revenue or use cash to pay those booked expenses in a different period, so net income isn't an accurate measure of cash flow. Remember from chapter 2 that profit and cash flow are not the same thing. Because financial statements are based on accrual-basis accounting, the statement of cash flows begins with an accrual-based calculation of net income. However, because the statement of cash flow is trying to determine *actual* cash flow from operations (cash actually received or disbursed, not booked), it must make adjustments to net income to get to an accurate amount.

On Austin's statement of cash flows, the first adjustment to net income is depreciation and amortization of $486,000. Why is this a positive adjustment to net income on the statement of cash flows? You will notice on the income statement that this same amount and title, depreciation and amortization of $486,000, is an expense, which reflects the decrease in value of certain assets over time. But this is a noncash expense. Austin's didn't have to pay someone $486,000. Therefore, it is added back to net income on the statement of cash flows, because this expense didn't require the use of cash.

Right after depreciation and amortization is a group of line items labeled "Change in operating assets and liabilities." These adjustments show changes year over year in some of the balance sheet accounts that may use or generate cash. Let's look at each line item. The first, accounts receivable of $61,000, reflects the reality that cash was generated by reducing receivables (collecting money owed to the company) from the prior year. If you look back to the balance sheet, you can see that Austin's receivables did decrease by $61,000 from 2011 to 2012. The inventories line item of negative $290,000 indicates that this amount of cash was spent to increase inventories. The accounts payable amount of $111,000 reflects the fact that, in growing the business, Austin's Cycle

Shop funded part of its growth by buying items on credit. Increasing accounts payable over the previous year was a source of $111,000 in cash. Income taxes payable of $165,000 indicates that Austin's income taxes have increased by this amount in the past year, but have not been paid, so is a source of cash. This same explanation applies to the next two line items, accrued payroll and related expenses, and other accrued liabilities. Since the amount of these obligations have increased from 2011 to 2012, but have not yet been paid, Austin's still has the use of the cash, which means they are reflected on the statement of cash flows as a source of cash.

At the end of the category, the summary entry "net cash provided by operating activities" is calculated by adding the positive (cash in) and negative (cash out) numbers. The net amount flowing into or out of the business is the total. In the Big Picture Breakdown at the beginning of the chapter, I explained how important this number is—the most important number on the sheet. Unless the company is very young, this number had better be positive. In the most current year, Austin's Cycle Shop's operating activities generated cash flow of $1.528 million, which bodes very well for the survival of the company.

For Austin's Cycle Shop, the trend is positive from 2010 to 2011, increasing 61 percent. But from 2011 to 2012 it decreases almost 25 percent. Part of your study of the financials would be to find out why cash flow from operations decreased in the past year. Two obvious causes are that cash was used to increase inventories and to prepay expenses.

The most important ratio to analyze here is the amount of cash flow generated from operating activities compared to profit (net income) for the same period. Calculating this for Austin's, we would divide the cash from operations by the net income ($1,528 divided by $1,087 = 1.4). You generally want this ratio to exceed 1.0, meaning you want cash flow to be greater than profit. Why? Because it reflects a company's ability to effectively turn profits into cash. Remember, a sale does not generate cash until it is collected. For 2010, 2011, and 2012, the cash flow/profit ratios are 1.8, 2.4, and 1.4, which reflects good cash generation. The ratio fell in 2012, which can be attributed to growth efforts, but Austin's will want to watch this trend carefully.

Cash Provided (or Used) by Investing Activities

After operating activities, the statement reveals cash flows from investing activities. Unlike cash flow from operations, which should be positive, healthy companies frequently use cash in investing activities, as does Austin's in each of the three years shown. For 2012, Austin's had net cash used in investing activities of $3.282 million, which is shown in parenthesis to indicate cash out or a use of cash. These negative numbers are typical and simply mean that management takes cash generated from operations (or financing activities) and invests more cash in assets. For example, Austin's used $1.410 million for capital expenditures, $1.217 million to purchase investments, and $655,000 for purchase of other assets.

When reviewing competitors' cash flow statements, take note of who is investing cash, buying assets, or even acquiring other companies to support future growth. A company growing well this year but not investing in its future growth will likely see growth slowing. In total, Austin's investing activities *used* cash of $3.282 million in 2012, $2.237 million in 2011, and $1.581 million in 2010. Austin and the board are investing more each year in order to support the growth of the business. A company with a positive amount here would be selling assets to generate cash, which is not sustainable. For example, a company could sell off one of its stores to generate cash, but would then have one less store. If a company continued this strategy they might end up with a lot of cash, but no stores and no retail business.

Cash Provided (or Used) by Financing Activities

Finally, the cash flow statement shows cash in and out from financing activities. This section reveals how a company is financing its business. Austin's issued stock to generate $1.801 million in cash. It also increased its long-tem debt (borrowed cash) by $200,000. If the company were to repay this money next year, it would be shown as negative $200,000, because cash would be used to reduce debt.

If the company is public, this section will show whether a company is paying a dividend and/or buying back stock. These are strategies that companies use to leverage their excess cash and provide value to stockholders. Dividend payments offer value in a very direct way, and a stock buyback makes the remaining shares worth more money (fewer shares means that each share is tied to a greater percentage of the company's earnings), thus raising the stock price. You'll see from Austin's cash flow statement that there is no line item for total dividends paid. The company is experiencing good growth, and therefore it is not surprising that it would not be paying a dividend. And although there is a line item for common stock repurchases, Austin's has not repurchased any shares in the last three years.

Understanding how the competition is funding its business or using excess cash is also useful. Are competing businesses borrowing money? Are they issuing or buying back stock? Are they paying a dividend? These are important questions to consider as you dive into a company's financing strategies. In the most recent year, Austin's financing activities generated cash of $2.001 million. And because this line item is growing we can assume that Austin's strategy to borrow more money and issue more stock is supporting strong growth plans.

Net Change in Cash and Cash Equivalents

Toward the bottom of the statement, you can see the increase in cash and cash equivalents for 2012 of $247,000. Remember the basic equation for this statement adds together the net increase or decrease in cash for the three categories combined.

Net cash from: operations + investing + financing =
increase or decrease in cash and cash equivalents

or

$$\$1,528 + (\$3,282) + \$2,001 = \$247$$

Of the three categories, cash provided from operations is the best way to generate cash. This reflects how the company's core operations are doing. Generating money by selling investments or assets is not sustainable. If cash is generated through borrowing, the company will have to pay it back in the future with interest.

Cash and Cash Equivalents at End of Year

The net change in cash is the amount—$247,000 for 2012—added to (or subtracted from) the cash and cash equivalents at the beginning of the year—$580,000—to create the *cash and cash equivalents at the end of the year*—$827,000, which is the last line item on a statement of cash flows, and the first line item on the balance sheet. Thus, the statement of cash flow tells the story of how Austin's ended up with $827,000 in the bank. Austin's cash has been increasing each year, which is generally positive because cash has grown as the company has grown. But there might be sound business reasons why a healthy company would have a reduction in cash balances in one year compared to the prior year. The statement of cash flows would give you clues as to why this happened.

The statement of cash flows helps us understand how a company is balancing its need to retain cash with its need to use cash to grow the business. It reveals how cash was used to further strategies that might change from year to year, just as the focus on particular drivers might shift over time.

INSIGHTS INTO THE STATEMENT OF CASH FLOWS

- The statement of cash flows measures cash generation.

- The cash flow statement basic equation is: Cash from (or used in) operating activities + Cash from (or used in) investing activities + Cash from (or used in) financing activities = Net change in cash. These also represent the key measures found on the statement.

- The three primary sources (and uses) of cash include operating activities, investing activities, and financing activities.

- The cash flow statement begins with net income from the income statement and makes adjustments to calculate cash flow, then ends with cash and cash equivalents, which is where the balance sheet begins.

- You want cash from operations, the most important number on the page, to increase each year. Cash balances might not increase because of other strategic uses of cash.

- Everything impacting profit and uses of cash also influences your cash flow statement, such as expense reduction and sales increase.

SECURING YOUR SEAT
AT THE TABLE

To know and not to do is not to know.
—Proverb

S o you've learned a bit about how your company functions and how to tell whether it's successfully growing and generating profit. What do you do now?

What I've provided here is just the foundation, a foundation you can turn into deep knowledge about how your company operates now and should operate in the future. Why go to the trouble? It's the best and fastest way to prove your worth and to secure a seat at the decision-making table, something that can make your work more rewarding and your career more successful.

Securing your seat at the table means adding value, developing and continuing to exercise your ability to influence decisions and decision-makers within your organization. You must study business generally, your business specifically, and then make and act upon sound decisions.

Your application of business acumen requires a focus on the chief concerns and goals of your boss or CEO. You'll need to develop and apply continued insights concerning market trends, competitor analysis, strategic choices, financial markets, consumer trends, and more. You'll need to communicate effectively using the 5 Key Drivers within the context of your company's strategic goals if you want to contribute to your company's growth, and to your own.

As you grow in your influence at the decision-making table, you'll need to stretch yourself, move outside your comfort zone. It can be challenging to find the time and energy, but the rewards will be worth it. Your knowledge and contributions will build your credibility, career, and company.

I challenge you to move forward with a commitment to *do it*.

In pursuing your personal or business objectives, you must never omit the hard work of preparation. An admiring audience member said to the virtuoso concert pianist, "I'd give my life to play like that." The predictable response: "I have."

SIX IDEAS FOR BUILDING BUSINESS ACUMEN

Here are six practical ideas to encourage and support your ongoing development and application of sound business acumen.

1. Commit the Time to Study and Research

Set aside time for regular study and research.

Your days are already full, crowded with professional and personal activities. Nevertheless, find opportunities to carve out the time to advance your credibility, your career, and your company. How much time do you spend watching television? Could you chat with coworkers less and read industry information more? Could you use your lunch time more productively? An hour of research even once a week will have a great payoff.

Whether you can spend an hour a week or a half-hour daily, set aside time for study and preparation—regularly. Then put it to use!

The Resources section in the back of this book offers a host of opportunities to learn more about business in general and your industry specifically. You can also sign up for our monthly newsletter or access other resources at www.seeingthebigpicture.com.

You should also devote time to learning how your company is organized and operates: its organization and internal structure, who the key officers are, your primary products and services, your present and future goals. Understand the important priorities, values, and strategies of your CEO, division head, and direct supervisor.

Do you know how your company is doing financially or what its financial goals are? Go deeper than the big picture of your company and explore the financials of each division or department if you can. How are the 5 Key Drivers being prioritized throughout your organization?

You can learn this by reading

- the annual report;

- e-mail and other communications from your boss and company officers;

- company press releases;

- materials on the company website;

- quarterly Form 10-Q filings and annual 10-K filings;

- and other resources about your company, including interviews of your senior leadership in all media. Ask your supervisor how to access additional internal operating data if it isn't readily available.

Also, if you are an employee of a public company, listen to your CEO's quarterly conference calls with Wall Street analysts. This quarterly call provides a current report on your company's operations and financial performance and your CEO's priorities and future plans. If you miss the actual call, an archived recording will likely be found on your company's website in the investor relations section.

You should also know who your three to four most important competitors are and learn their basic financial data, strategies, products and services, and strengths and weaknesses. Read their annual reports, their websites, and information about them in the media.

Finally, learn what is happening in the external environment that might affect your company. Read or listen to financial, economic, and business news from websites and print and broadcast media, including books, magazines, the *Wall Street Journal*, and the business section of any large metropolitan daily paper.

As Harold S. Geneen, once CEO of ITT and father of the international conglomerate, once said, "When you have mastered numbers, you will in fact no longer be reading numbers, any more than you read words when reading books. You will be reading meanings."

2. Talk with Key Company Managers

Build relationships with key leaders and managers at your company. Start with your boss or supervisor. Talk regularly with peers or teammates in different departments who have specific expertise. Ask questions that reveal your own research. Share your helpful insights in return.

Talk with your boss or supervisor about the big picture of your organization and how your team or department, and you personally, can have a more significant impact.

Learn the key measures and "dashboard metrics" that your boss and your division's or company's senior management are focused on. Discuss with your supervisor how you can better achieve these targets so you know how your team, and your job function, fit in.

Setting up these discussions need not be complicated or overly formal; meet people for lunch, or set brief appointments in their offices.

Let your reasons be known: you want to become more knowledgeable in order to make more effective contributions.

Build relationships!

3. Be Proactive—Contribute and Follow Through

Whenever an assignment or opportunity for action results from your study, discussions, or meetings, follow through and *do it*. Report back in a timely way to the appropriate parties so others will realize you have *done it!*

When realistic or appropriate, put your comments and questions into succinct, meaningful, and timely e-mails or memos addressed to appropriate personnel. However, don't overwhelm people with a flood of ideas or recommendations. Be targeted in your approach.

Draw up a brief written action list concerning any or all of the 5 Key Drivers. Link your actions to results that "move the needle" in areas important to your boss and senior management and that support the key measures they have identified. Identify in writing how your actions impact the drivers. Give a copy to your boss or supervisor and discuss.

4. Attend Industry Meetings and Make Outside Contacts

If your company provides any occasion for you to attend industry conferences or major customer meetings, take the opportunity. Network with those you meet there. Read the literature available. Grow your own database of contacts. Keep in touch with them over time, as possible. Gain your own direct sources of helpful industry, economic, or business information. Stay in communication with those you meet.

5. Find a Mentor

Ask a coworker—maybe a peer or senior manager—to work with and mentor you. Your partner should be someone to whom you can make a commitment regarding your business acumen action plan and to whom you can be accountable. That person may want to further his or her own knowledge, and you can help and support each other. *Being* a mentor to someone else will help you both.

Above all, be accountable to *yourself* in your assignment to see your company's big picture and continue developing your business acumen.

6. Influence Management

To influence senior management, you have to follow all of the above recommendations as you prepare yourself to present an idea or opportunity.

Then, when asking a leader to consider seriously your views or recommendations, follow these four important suggestions—principles that have worked for thousands of employees across many industries and types of companies:

Listen to understand: Listen first. Your sole purpose in listening? To *understand* where the individual or management team is coming from, to get what's important to *them*. In every meeting, listen carefully for opportunities to ask insightful questions and learn even more. If you deeply understand *their* point of view, *their* needs and priorities, it will first influence you. Then you'll be better equipped to influence them.

Present their case and needs to them: Once you have listened deeply, make a "my understanding of your needs and objectives" summary before making your own proposals. Once managers know that you really do understand their perspective, they will be more open to listening to your analysis and proposals. You'll have built greater trust.

Speak their language: Once you've established mutual understanding, connect your analysis and recommendations to their strategic goals, concerns, and needs. Link your message to what's important to them, in financial language they understand. Demonstrate the impact of your proposal or analysis on those drivers important to them. Remember that every department or function has differing priorities.

Use ROI analysis: Ultimately, every business decision boils down to determining how best to use cash for maximum return on investment. Make a convincing case for a favorable ROI through your recommendation. (Refer to chapter 3 for more on ROI, or go to www.seeingthebigpicture.com to download a more complete explanation of calculating return on investment.)

YOUR VALUE ADDED

Your ultimate ability to become a more valuable, and valued, employee is primarily up to you. Your contribution to the success of your department, division, or company will add to your own success. Helping others along the way will add dimensions of experience, knowledge, and insight that will benefit both them and you.

As you become better known for your insightful business acumen, you will become more credible as a contributor and more valued as a member of your company, thus building your career. Wherever your career takes you, your ability to understand and implement the 5 Key Drivers and to exercise the acumen associated with them will lead to sustained success.

I encourage your continued commitment and hard work. Persevere. I'm confident it will pay off!

THE BEGINNING OF MY STORY

When I first got out of college, I began my career in banking. I will always remember my enthusiasm and my desire to excel in my first job after college, to set the organization on fire with the sheer brilliance of my performance.

Well, as it turned out, I created more smoke than fire. I quickly realized how little I had actually learned in school. I struggled even to keep up a stumbling pace with my associates who had spent just a few years in the real world.

I remember how there was nothing more discouraging than being dressed for success and feeling like a failure—sitting in a meeting with managers and senior executives, totally in over my head, trying to follow basic concepts of the financial discussion.

I was usually at a loss to make any intelligent comments, much less any meaningful contribution. I regularly found myself hoping that no one would call on me for anything important, in case I actually had to say something and reveal that I had only faint clues as to what they were talking about.

So, early in my career, the embarrassment of ignorance compelled me to make a commitment to competence.

There is no more empowering feeling in business than that of being in the company of experienced leaders and being able not only to follow the flow of their discussion but to make intelligent contributions to it. There's nothing like sitting in an important meeting with colleagues and managers and having everyone nod his or her head in acknowledgment of your insightful comments and recommendations.

I wrote this book simply to educate and encourage you. Please believe me when I say, "If I can do it, *you* can do it!" Really! Anyone can build business acumen. The key will be to move forward, adopting Nike's slogan at face value. *Just do it!*

Whatever your background, schooling, or experience, there is nothing about the 5 Key Drivers that is beyond your grasp.

I sincerely hope that you will make a commitment to building your business acumen through ongoing study and action. Continue to use this book as a reference guide, a resource.

The ultimate key? To *engage.* My very best wishes for your success, and my encouragement once more to stay with it! Remember . . .

What lies behind us and what lies before us are tiny matters compared to what lies within us.
—Proverb

RESOURCES

Books

David Allen (2001): *Getting Things Done: The Art of Stress-Free Productivity*

Larry Bossidy, Ram Charan, and Charles Burck (2002): *Execution: The Discipline of Getting Things Done*

Marcus Buckingham and Curt Coffman (1999): *First, Break All the Rules: What the World's Greatest Managers Do Differently*

Dale Carnegie (1937): *How to Win Friends and Influence People*

Jim Collins (2001): *Good to Great: Why Some Companies Make the Leap . . . and Others Don't*

Jim Collins and Jerry I. Porras (1997/2002): *Built to Last: Successful Habits of Visionary Companies*

Stephen R. Covey (1989/2004): *The 7 Habits of Highly Effective People: Powerful Lessons in Personal Change*

Stephen M. R. Covey (2006): *The Speed of Trust: The One Thing That Changes Everything*

Peter F. Drucker (1967/2002): *The Effective Executive: The Definitive Guide to Getting the Right Things Done*

Thomas L. Friedman (2005): *The World Is Flat: A Brief History of the Twenty-First Century*

Atul Gawande (2009): *The Checklist Manifesto: How to Get Things Right*

Michael Gerber (1995/2001): *The E-Myth Revisited: Why Most Small Businesses Don't Work and What to Do About It*

Chip and Dan Heath (2010): *Switch: How to Change Things When Change Is Hard*

John C. Maxwell (1998/2007 [rev. ed.]): *The 21 Irrefutable Laws of Leadership: Follow Them and People Will Follow You*

Magazines and Newspapers

Business Week and BusinessWeek.com

Fast Company and FastCompany.com

Forbes and Forbes.com

Fortune and Fortune.com

Harvard Business Review and hbr.org

Investor's Business Daily

Smart Money and SmartMoney.com

Wall Street Journal and wsj.com

Local newspaper business section or local financial newspaper

Websites

CEOExpress.com

Finance.Google.com

Finance.Yahoo.com

Hoovers.com

MoneyCentral.msn.com

Nasdaq.com

Reuters.com

SEC.gov

Individual business websites

ACKNOWLEDGMENTS

"If I have seen further, it is by standing on the shoulders of giants."
—Sir Isaac Newton

I was always in love with the idea of writing a book . . . until I started writing a book. The idea of it was much easier than the actual effort. I could not have done it without support from my friends who made giant contributions.

- My assistant and business manager Sharon Biegler has been with me from the beginning . . . she is the glue that holds everything together.

- Keith Gulledge who got me going.

- Mike Wright who kept me going.

- Stephen M.R. Covey, a great thinker, leader, and mentor, and Jeri Covey, a wise sounding board.

- Pam Walsh, a fantastic coach who believes in me, yet keeps my feet on the ground.

- And talk about a team who sees the big picture—special thanks to the talented Lari Bishop and her colleagues at Greenleaf Book Group.

This book, from its concepts to its individual character, is the result of some of my talented friends at Acumen Learning, including Brent Barclay, Ryan Barclay, Dave Butler, Steve Call, Ben Cook, Jeff Cope, Ben Croshaw, Becca Edwards, Ryan Hunt, Greg Kandare, Shayne Keckley, Ben Penrod, Randy Porter, Christian Purnell, Jason Richards,

Kenny Snarr, Ryan Stirland, and Mark Wood. This team performs an amazing amount of amazingly important work for our clients day-in and day-out. While bad business practices and bad business behavior dominate much of the news, I find that the vast majority of businesses and business leaders are doing great things. It is an honor to have partnered with great organizations including eighteen of the Fortune 50 and to have worked closely with so many capable and commendable people, who just so happen to work in business. We have the best clients, and we hope they learn as much from us as we learn from them.

I have many brilliant colleagues who have offered advice and unending support. In particular, my thanks to Paul Brockbank, Kim Capps, Ram Charan, Craig Christensen, David Covey, Ken Evans, Joe Folkman, Amy Green-Williams, Joseph Grenny, Jeff Hill, Rich Hill, Randy Illig, Gary Judd, Greg Link, Stephan Mardyks, Rod Morely, Gabe Williams, and Jack Zenger.

I have been blessed with great parents, Lloyd and Kathleen Cope, who have always been there and who have relentlessly cheered me on.

And most of all, I thank God daily for my wife Karen, our children Austin and his wife Brittany, Spencer, Ryan and his wife Michelle, Conner, Isabella, Noelle and my three grandchildren. I could fill volumes expressing my love and admiration for each one of you. I am humbled to be part of your lives.

ABOUT THE AUTHOR

Kevin Cope is not only a successful executive, he is also a trusted resource and confidant to business leaders from around the world and a sought-after keynote speaker. For over twenty-five years, Kevin has promoted the idea that the brightest minds in business understand the essence of how a company makes money, and they use this knowledge to make good things happen for the company. In other words, they have strong business acumen.

Recognizing that business acumen is not only essential, but also lacking in many organizations, in 2002 Kevin founded Acumen Learning, a training company that has gone on to teach Kevin's ideas and business models to some of the world's most respected and successful companies. Kevin's specialty is teaching businesspeople—no matter their role and no matter their experience—how to look at business through the lens of 5 Business Drivers (cash, profit, assets, growth, and people) and use the financials to measure progress. Kevin believes that businesspeople must set and achieve goals and obtain results in these five areas in order to achieve the most important objective for any company: long-term, sustainable profitability in support of its mission.

Please visit www.seeingthebigpicture.com to learn more about Kevin and his ideas.

ABOUT ACUMEN LEARNING

We educate and inspire individuals and organizations by Building their Business Acumen, thus accelerating their ability to accomplish great results. This inspires us and we are enjoying the journey!

THE BIG PICTURE

Acumen Learning has tested over 100,000 employees working for some of the most recognizable companies in the world. We have found that while most employees understand their function really well—they know their responsibilities as an IT professional, or they are really smart as an operations manager, etc.—90 percent of them don't understanding important business measures. Those who do understand these business and financial concepts (typically C-level executives and the finance department) often struggle to communicate their knowledge with stakeholders and employees with clarity and in an engaging way.

This lack of understanding, clarity, and engagement results in leaders who struggle to align their team's actions and strategy with corporate results, departments that are too insular, and organizations that scramble when it comes to turning increased complexity into financial advantage. Employees within these organizations lack the understanding and conviction to explain what they need to do in clear, simple terms, and how their team, or organization will improve the company's moneymaking process. This leads to a lack of engagement and a feeling of being disconnected. The results are employees who shy away from making important business decisions, employees who make uninformed business decisions, or employees who slow down the decision making process in an effort to avoid making the wrong choice.

Since its founding in 2002, Acumen Learning's 5 Drivers business model and financial strategies have been field tested with more than one hundred thousand people in over thirty countries and at eighteen of the Fortune 50—developing businesspeople who can see the big picture without losing sight of the details, who can cut through complexity and conquer uncertainty, and who consistently make the right strategic bets that deliver clear and measurable business results. In short, our business acumen training, web sessions, and keynotes will help you develop not just smarter people, but smarter businesspeople.

BUILDING BUSINESS ACUMEN® TRAINING, WEB SESSIONS, AND KEYNOTES

Think about it, you can spend your training dollars on everything from communication skills to management techniques and end up with great leaders who don't know whether their efforts are good, bad, or indifferent when it comes to achieving profitable and sustainable growth. Business acumen training from Acumen Learning will provide needed clarity and will teach employees how to leverage their leadership skills to strengthen their company's financial position. Every department from operations to sales, and every role from an up-and-coming manager to a seasoned executive will clearly see how they can practice and perfect their business acumen to build their credibility, their career, and their company.

If you are interested in business acumen training for your team, we're ready when you are.

Contact Acumen Learning:

801-224-5444

info@acumenlearning.com

www.acumenlearning.com

You can read our free newsletter at www.acumenlearning.com/subscribe.

INDEX